HOW TO BUILD A

How To Build A
HOT ROD

Dennis W. Parks

MOTORBOOKS
INTERNATIONAL

This edition first published in 2003 by Motorbooks International, an imprint of MBI Publishing Company, Galtier Plaza, Suite 200, 380 Jackson Street, St. Paul, MN 55101-3885 USA

The information in this book is true and complete to the best of our knowledge. All recommendations are made without any guarantee on the part of the author or Publisher, who also disclaim any liability incurred in connection with the use of this data or specific details.

We recognize that some words, model names and designations, for example, mentioned herein are the property of the trademark holder. We use them for identification purposes only. This is not an official publication.

Motorbooks International titles are also available at discounts in bulk quantity for industrial or sales-promotional use. For details write to Special Sales Manager at Motorbooks International Wholesalers & Distributors, Galtier Plaza, Suite 200, 380 Jackson Street, St. Paul, MN 55101-3885 USA.

Library of Congress Cataloging-in-Publication Data

Parks, Dennis, 1959-
    How to build a hot rod / Dennis W. Parks
      p cm. -- (Motorbooks workshop)
    ISBN 0-7603-1304-0 (pbk. : alk. paper)
     1. Hot rods--Design and construction. I. Title. II. Series.

TL255 .P363 2003
629.228'6--dc21

Edited by Peter Bodensteiner
Designed by Chris Fayers

Printed in Hong Kong

Acknowledgments

I would like to thank several people for making this book possible. Thank you to Keith Moritz at Morfab Customs for allowing me to take up so much of his time to photograph many of the garage scenes. Thank you to Chris Clarke for all of his technical assistance in the past, present, and future.

Thanks also go to Roger Ward for all of his moral support throughout the years. Most of all, I want to thank my bride, Sandy, for allowing me to dream and for doing all she can to make those dreams come true.

To all of the above, plus all of the companies who supplied photos and technical information, a very sincere thank you.

Dennis W. Parks

Dedication

To Sandy with love.

CONTENTS

CHAPTER 1
WHAT TO BUILD?

Deciding whether you want to build a hot rod is easy. Either you do or you don't, and if you are reading this, you probably already want to. The toughest part is choosing what to build. A few decades ago, this decision would have been much easier. You would scour the salvage yards and classified ads until you found something that sparked your interest and was within your budget. (Of course, this is still a great way to find a hot rod, whether you are looking for an already completed rod, an older project that needs new life, or an abandoned project.)

Today, there is also a vast assortment of reproduction bodies and chassis on the market that can make the decision on what to build almost overwhelming. Although it would be virtually impossible to reproduce all of the various body styles that may be considered hot rod material, the currently available selection should give you plenty from which to choose.

For the purposes of this book, we will use the term "hot rod" to describe any automobile originally manufactured in the United States prior to 1949 that has been modified. We

Without a doubt, one of the most popular body styles for a hot rod is the 1932 Ford roadster. This dark blue example includes an independent front suspension, smooth hood sides, and large-diameter billet wheels.

More of a traditional example is this 1932 Ford roadster that uses a dropped front axle, chopped windshield, louvered hood sides, hairpin radius rods, and Halibrand wheels.

Very popular among rodders is the 1932 Ford five-window coupe. This traditional example features a polished four-link front suspension, dropped axle, and lots of louvers. Three-window coupes from 1933–1934 are also very popular; they lack the tiny side window.

Leading the list of popular sedans is the 1933–1934 Ford Tudor. This classy specimen is full fendered and very smooth, and it has room for four adults.

will also include vehicles that are reproductions of those cars. Some of these manufacturers are still in business today, and some are mere memories. You'll see plenty of hot rods manufactured by Ford/Lincoln, General Motors, and Chrysler, as well as Nash, Studebaker, and LaSalle. By our definition, there are many other possibilities too. Some are just more common than others, for reasons such as numbers produced and how much attention the aftermarket has paid to certain models. As more rodders build a certain make or model of vehicle, the aftermarket grows to meet that demand. At the same time, the parts the aftermarket produces influence which vehicles rodders choose to build. As the aftermarket grows by making more parts available, more rodders build that type of vehicle. For example, at one time, no self-respecting rodder would consider building a 1937 Ford, so originals were cast off as junk,

This Willys coupe and Ford sedan give a glimpse of the variety of hot rods. The 1937 Ford sedan with the wide whitewall tires in the background represents the milder side of hot rodding, while the blown Willys in the foreground suggests the wilder side.

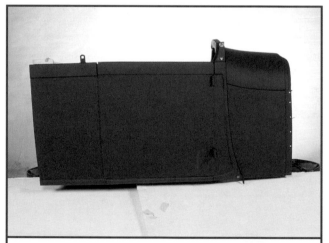

Available in steel is this 1930–1931 Ford Model A roadster pickup cab. With or without fenders, one of these roadster pickups features a great fun/build expense ratio. Brookville Roadsters

One of the veterans of the fiberglass street rod body business is Wescott's Auto Restyling. Besides steel-reinforced fiberglass bodies, Wescott's manufactures other fiberglass parts such as fenders, dash panels, and splash aprons.

until Gibbon Fiberglass Reproductions started producing those bodies in fiberglass. The fiberglass company knew that rodders wanted something different, while rodders knew that new fiberglass was easier to build than resurrecting an original. As they say, timing is everything.

Some people may wonder how hot rodders established the 1948/1949 "cutoff." It is probably more of a design viewpoint than anything else. For the most part, all cars originally built prior to the 1949 model year had running boards. When the "new" models came out in 1949,

running boards were gone. "New" vehicles were much more aerodynamic (at least by the standards of the day).

CHOOSING A YEAR, MAKE, AND MODEL

Choosing what to build is largely based on two things: what is available and what you like. If you are looking to build a Ford-based hot rod, you are in luck for almost any year and body style that you may desire. Not that every year and body style is being reproduced in fiberglass, but there are several more for Fords than for any other manufacturer.

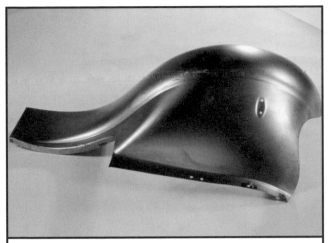

Original steel fenders are notorious for cracking and tearing, so Brookville Roadsters makes these steel replacement 1928–1929 Ford front fenders. Brookville Roadsters

These steel rear fenders make the perfect companion to replacement steel front fenders. Brookville Roadsters

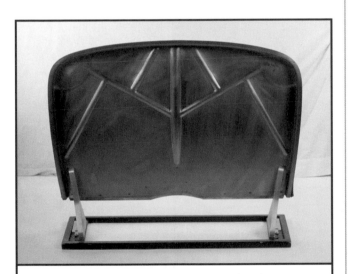

With uncut originals being very rare and therefore expensive, Brookville Roadsters is making its own example of the 1932 Ford firewall in steel. Brookville Roadsters

Various Chevrolet, Dodge, Plymouth, and Willys bodies are available in reproduction form; however, the variety is limited compared to those for Ford. Reproduction fenders, running boards, deck lids, and hoods are easier to find for all models than complete bodies.

"Slender" fenders (1928–1934)
Cars that are hot rod material can be divided into two categories: those with "slender" fenders and those with "fat" fenders. Although the actual years may vary

somewhat from one manufacturer to another, cars manufactured up through the mid-1930s were originally equipped with fenders that basically just covered the top and back of the wheel and tire. Later cars utilized fenders that wrapped around the wheel and tire more closely and that were more of an integral part of the body. During the early days of hot rodding, these later cars were undesirable due to the excessive bulk and weight. In the 1980s, rodders began to realize that these "fat" cars needed love too.

Slender-fendered cars quickly gained fame with hot rodders. Relatively lightweight even in stock trim, these cars could be further lightened if rodders removed the fenders and running boards. When you are considering power-to-weight ratios, more power moves less weight faster. If you are going to be racing your hot rod, this is important. If you are not racing, it is mostly just an aesthetic decision, although it could be a financial one as you add the cost of the fenders, the time involved in fitting them, and the cost and time in painting.

Whether you use the fenders or not, the older cars are also smaller than their younger cousins. Realizing this ahead of time may make your buying decision easier if you are planning to build a hot rod to haul the entire family. For the most part, two adults in the front seat and two adults in the back seat is about the limit in a slender-fendered hot rod.

"Fat" fenders (1935–1948)
Fat-fendered rods are usually roomier than their earlier counterparts. Although many hot rods may never see two

These two hot rods are good examples of slender- and fat-fendered rods. The 1932 Ford Vicky in the foreground has "slender" fenders that mostly cover only the tops of the tires. The 1938 Ford coupe in the background features "fat" fenders that wrap more closely around the wheel and tire, as well as the tops.

This photo illustrates two points: the difference in three-window and five-window coupes, and fenders versus no fenders. The black full-fendered 1934 is a three-window (one on each side and one back) and has longer doors. The yellow highboy is a five-window (two on each side and one back) and has a shorter door.

adults in either seat, a third could ride without cramping anyone very much. With the additional room found in a fat-fendered car, it will also be somewhat easier to install all of the creature comforts that we now take for granted. Air conditioning, stereo, and power steering can also go into an earlier car; however, proper planning will become even more important as you attempt to put all of the same goodies in a smaller space.

With more room comes more expense. It is safe to say that for every fendered 1932 Ford hot rod, there is another 1932 Ford hot rod that is running without fenders. If you are building a 1940 Ford, however, you are going to need the fenders and running boards, or the car is going to look like something is missing. True, there are a few examples of some fat-fendered cars that were built into hot rods without fenders; however, they are relatively few.

Some people will say that real hot rods don't have fenders. The highboy roadster looks the part of a hot rod, while the fendered Vicky looks calm. More than likely, the two cars have similar drivetrains.

The limited backseat room in a Model A Ford led the builder of this 1929 Tudor to remove the rear seat and add a rear delivery door. This provides better access for luggage and coolers.

RELATIVE COSTS OF REPRO PARTS FOR VEHICLES OF VARIOUS YEARS

Because the cars suitable for hot rodding are over half a century old, NOS (new old stock) parts for them are getting pretty scarce—and none too cheap. On the other hand, I can look up the price for a repro fiberglass fender in any of a number of catalogs. If you happen to have a set of NOS fenders that will fit on that abandoned project that you brought home from the swap meet, you are a step ahead of the game. Otherwise, if those fenders are dented, cracked, and rusty, some repro parts may be a good investment.

Some parts of a hot rod are going to cost the same, no matter what they go on. When comparing the same sizes, tires will cost the same whether they are going on a fender-less Model A Ford or a fat-fendered Oldsmobile. Likewise, a nicely detailed, carbureted small block Chevrolet engine

In the early days of hot rodding, these fat-fendered rods were thought to be useless. That has all changed, as they are quite popular today. Whether they are at "stock" height or slammed on the ground, these fat-fendered rods look good.

Though it is purely an assumption, the ride height of this primered hot rod is probably adjusted with air bags. An air bag suspension allows you to raise the vehicle to a comfortable driving level, then lower it for that supercool stance while at your destination. The fat fenders help conceal the air suspension components.

is going to cost the same, no matter what it is supplying power to.

What will make a significant difference in the overall cost to build a hot rod is the year and body style you choose. The table on page 16 shows the costs for reproduction Ford chassis and a wide variety of reproduction Ford bodies. To make this a fair comparison, the chassis prices are all from one leading manufacturer. Likewise, the body prices are all from one leading manufacturer to eliminate

differences due to manufacturer rather than vehicle make and style. These manufacturers are not necessarily the most expensive and they are certainly not the only manufacturer of the parts listed.

Although more aftermarket products are designed for Ford hot rods than any other, a variety of companies manufacture chassis and bodies for other marques. These companies seem to be more of a niche, sticking to a somewhat limited body style or brand. These companies

Are you looking for a "gennie" steel fender or other nonrepro item for your hot rod project? Swap meets are the best place to look for those original items. Major rodding events such as the NSRA Street Rod Nationals or the Goodguys Rod & Custom Nationals usually have a large swap meet vendor turnout.

Most large swap meets will have at least a few "complete cars" for sale. These usually include the frame, body panels, original suspension, and drivetrain. The suspension and drivetrain will usually end up going in the dumpster, but the body and frame should be worthy of repair. If you are looking for something unique for your next project, this may be a place to start, as the vendors usually don't want to haul these cars back home.

usually do offer the chassis and the body, allowing you to purchase the two largest components from one source if you desire. Some of these other available repro hot rods are listed in the table on page 16.

CHOOSING A BODY STYLE

For some people, nothing but a roadster would do for their hot rod, while others may prefer a coupe. Still other hot rodders may not care what they build, as long as it's a 1932

Ford. If you haven't made the decision yet, read on for further information on the many body styles to choose from.

What is available

Unless you are a master metalsmith or accomplished with any of a variety of composite materials, you should probably stick with a body style that is still available in decent numbers, or one that is being reproduced today. Some extremely accomplished metalsmiths are making phantom

TABLE 1				
Chassis	**1928–1931**	**1932**	**1933–1934**	**1935–1948**
Economy chassis (a perimeter frame with all brackets welded on, but no suspension hardware included)	$1,698 (straight axle)	$2,740 (straight axle)	$2,678 (straight axle)	$3,317 (independent front suspension)
Complete chassis (complete chassis, except for wheels and tires)	$5,035 (straight axle)	$6,298 (straight axle)	$6,298 (straight axle)	$6,298 (independent front suspension)
Body Style	Body only/body package[1]	Body only/body package[1]	Body only/body package[1]	Body only/body package[1]
Roadster	$5,590/$6,440	$5,590/$6,790	$5,590/$7,340	N/A*
Convertible/Cabriolet[2]	N/A[3]	$6,500/$7,700/$1,900[4]	N/A[3]	$7,400/$8,550/$2,350[4]
Roadster Pickup	$3,390/$3,955	$3,390/$4,100/$1,550[5]	$3,390/$4,900/$1,550[5]	N/A[3]
3 Window Coupe	N/A*	$6,700/$7,900	$6,700/$8,450	N/A[3]
5 Window Coupe	N/A[3]	$6,950/$8,150	N/A[3]	N/A[3]
Tudor Sedan	N/A*	$6,650/$7,850	$6,650/$8,400	N/A[3]
Sedan Delivery	N/A[3]	$7,200/$8,400	$6,650/$8,400	N/A*
Tudor Phaeton	$5,590/$6,600	N/A[3]	N/A*	N/A*
Fordor Phaeton	N/A[3]	$7,250/$8,050/$1,450[4]	$7,450/$9,075/$1,295[4]	N/A*

[1] Body package includes body, fenders, and running boards. [2] Cabriolets and convertibles both have folding top and side windows. [3] Not available from this particular manufacturer; however, known to be available from other manufacturers. [4] Third price shown is for hardware for folding top (top material not included). [5] Third price shown is for repro pickup bed. * Unknown if this model is currently available in reproduction.

TABLE 2	
1934–1935 Chevrolet	**1940–1941 Willys**
Chassis, $2,855/$5,425	Chassis, $3,294/$3,955
3-Window Coupe body package, $5,500	Coupe body package, $10,155
Roadster body package, $5,300	
Cabriolet body package, $5,550	
Victoria Delivery body package, $7,250	

body styles based on older vehicles; however, their talent is far beyond the scope of this book. Searching through rod magazine ads, numerous catalogs, and the Internet, you will find a wide variety of body styles from which to choose—quite possibly, too many to choose from without making some additional decisions as to what you really want from your hot rod.

Original manufacturer The majority of hot rods are based on cars that were originally manufactured by General Motors, Ford Motor Company, or Chrysler Corporation. Other brand hot rods do exist, but they are few by comparison. If you are seriously looking to build a hot rod based on an authentic pre-1948 car, try to acquire all of the seemingly nonimportant stuff when you obtain the bulk of your new project. Such items as dash trim, fender brackets, and window riser mechanisms may be hard to come by later

if you are building anything other than a Ford-based hot rod. Although some rodders may be bored with Ford, there is no denying that more aftermarket parts are available for Ford-based hot rods than any other brand. Even if you are able to build anything that you may need for your nonmainstream hot rod, at least having a stock part to use as a pattern will ultimately save you time and trouble.

Phantom body styles Most reproduction bodies are obviously reproductions of cars that were built by major automakers years ago. However, some of the companies in the hot rod body manufacturing business have taken the liberty of designing "new" or "phantom" body styles that the original manufacturers didn't offer. For instance, Ford Motor Company never produced a three-window coupe in 1937. Yet two companies, Downs and Minotti, are each making their own version of a 1937 Ford three-window coupe. The two bodies share the basic characteristics and body lines of their "authentic" cousins, yet they have some subtle differences.

Closed car

Another method for dividing hot rod body styles is by whether (perhaps it should be weather) the car is open or closed. In other words, does it have a top? This is probably one of the most important decisions to consider when you are considering building a hot rod. Do you want to be subjected to the elements while enjoying your hot rod, or

Most any 1932 Ford can be listed as a favorite. This Tudor sedan has a front seat and a backseat, and thus it can haul four people comfortably.

Want to haul four people but want an open car? This phaeton, available in two- and four-door models, provides room and fresh air.

Although roadsters had ceased production by the mid-1930s, open-air driving became available with a Cabriolet. The top could be up or down, but the doors included roll-up windows, making them truly different from a roadster.

When choosing a hot rod project, don't forget to consider pickup trucks or other commercial vehicles. This 1940 Ford pickup would be welcome in most any rodder's garage. On most originals, the bed is beaten up quite a bit, but new bed panels are available.

do you always want to be dry, warm, cool, and comfortable? When you are driving across the state or the country to a rod run, it may be nice to turn on the air conditioning (or the heater) and the stereo for a while without wind and the elements rushing in. Give this one some thought. You will be glad you did.

Coupe Rivaled perhaps only by roadsters, coupes are typically what comes to mind when someone imagines a hot rod. Smaller than a sedan body, a little coupe with a big engine has a way of shouting "hot rod." Some are hotter than others, but most any pre-1949 coupe can easily be considered hot rod material.

For most coupes, seating capacity is going to be limited to two, or possibly three in the later models. Some coupes do have back seats, and some have rumble seats (instead of a trunk); however, in either case, legroom is going to be limited. Business coupes typically have more interior room

Above: *Although this one has been massaged quite a bit, Lincoln Zephyrs were available on showroom floors years ago.* Right: *If you dare to be different, you can gain attention by building something like this early-1930s Studebaker. Note the headlights are behind doors in the front fenders.*

Ford Motor Company didn't make a three-window coupe in 1937, but they are popular today due to phantom bodies made by a couple of different fiberglass companies. Available from Downs and Minotti, these fiberglass phantoms never rust.

19

Looking back to an earlier time is this superslick 1933 Ford coupe. Gold pearl paint, lots of chrome, and wide whitewall tires on polished wheels would have identified this car as belonging to a "bucks up" rodder in the 1950s and 1960s.

Rumble seats were a popular option on early Fords. Eliminating the trunk, the extra passenger space necessitates stepping on the fender or bumper to get in or out. Note the step pad on the rear fender.

than other coupes and are therefore better candidates for a custom-built rear seat than a standard coupe.

A coupe's limited seating capacity would be the major drawback if you were building a hot rod for the entire family to enjoy at a rod run. A small trailer could be used for hauling the lawn chairs, coolers, and other stuff, but the drive could be less than pleasant for any backseat

passengers. If this hot rod is typically just going to haul one or two people, the trunk should be plenty big enough for a cooler and a suitcase for those out-of-state jaunts.

Sedan Practicality is what has made so many sedans popular among rodders. Having two seats, a sedan is practically a necessity if you plan to haul the family to a rod run

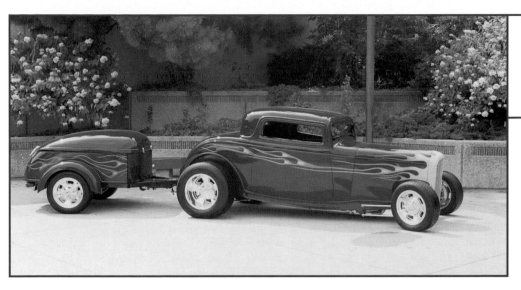

Although the trailer shown is small in appearance, it is quite large in capacity compared to the trunk space of the car pulling it.

Perhaps the best thing about a Sedan is the additional room available for hauling everthing while on these cross-country rod runs.

The stock bulge in the back of this sedan provides a bit more storage space in the trunk. These are commonly referred to as "humpback" sedans.

Without the bulge and therefore sporting a flat back, these sedans are sometimes referred to as "slant back" sedans.

The rear side panel on a sedan delivery makes a great place to advertise your business or your obsession. With the rear delivery door, access to the back of the car is greatly improved.

or cruise night. Depending on the make and model (and of course the size of your passengers), you can sit two or three people in front, along with two or three in back, so the whole family can be cruisin' in style.

Some sedans may not have a trunk at all, while those that do will be reduced in size by the presence of the rear seat. Everything is a tradeoff. For distant rod runs or family picnics, a trailer may be necessary to haul a spare tire, tools, or lawn chairs, but if the entire family can go, the extra trouble may be worth it.

If you are going to be traveling alone, or with just one other person, but need or desire to have some extra room, a sedan delivery may be a wise choice. The rear delivery door makes access to the back of the car much more convenient than crawling over the seats, and in an emergency could serve as a place to sleep. "I thought *you* made the hotel reservations!"

Open car

Even though your roadster/convertible/cabriolet may have a top, it is still considered an open car. If you can put the top down (or remove it completely), it is an open car. If you live in a sunny-all-the-time climate, an open car may be just right for you to consider as a hot rod. If that is not the case, but you want an open car anyway, your rod running season may be shorter, or you will

This Model A roadster on Deuce rails features a removable, nonfolding hard top. Hard tops are snug and sturdy, but they lack the convenience and versatility of a fold-down top.

What looks like a 1934 Ford roadster is actually a cabriolet. The difference is that the cabriolet has roll-up windows.

This cabriolet is a highly stylized version of a 1939 Ford, as manufactured by Coast to Coast. Sectioning the body brings the fenders high up in relationship to the body.

learn to deal with Mother Nature. Rod and custom painter extraordinaire Roger Ward summed it up when he said, "Whether it's hot or cold, you will always be cool in a roadster."

Roadster For all intents and purposes, roadsters are about the same as coupes, except that they don't have a hard top. Well, okay, they may have a removable hard top…but they don't have roll-up side windows. No matter what *anybody* tells you, a true roadster does not have side glass. If it does, the car in question is actually a cabriolet. Zippered or snap-on side curtains can be utilized to keep out the elements on a roadster. Well-designed windwings mounted on the side of the windshield also work wonders yet provide the "open air" feeling that roadster owners love so much.

Cabriolet/Convertible If you desire to have an open car yet choose to be isolated from the elements when Mother Nature rears her sometimes angry head, a cabriolet or a convertible may be what you need. With a removable or fold-down top, you can cruise in style with the wind blowing through your hair and the sun warming your skin. Should it start raining, not only can you put the top up, but you can roll up the side windows as well for a warm, dry ride. Of course, with a cabriolet or a convertible, you can drive to an event with the air conditioning on and then put the top down while cruising around town for the ultimate in coolness.

Fendered or highboy

After deciding what year and body style you want to build as a hot rod, you may need to ask yourself if it should have

A very popular highboy candidate is the 1933–1934 Ford coupe. These cars just seem to be destined to be hot rods, whether sporting a traditional suspension, or a high-tech independent front and/or rear suspension as in this example.

This is basically the same car, except with fenders and scallops. With or without fenders, these coupes make great hot rods.

fenders or not. For some people, this may not be a relevant question, while for others, it may not be relevant for just the opposite reason. If you are leaning toward a fat-fendered hot rod, you probably would not even think about building it sans fenders. On these cars, the fenders were an integral design component of the car, so to remove them would look absurd.

On the other hand, if you are contemplating building a slender-fendered rod, you have more to think about. Part of your decision will be based on the image or concept that you want to express with your hot rod. If you are building a lakes racer–inspired rod, it would be only natural to leave the fenders off. A nostalgia rod can go either way, depending on what era and locale you consider truly nostalgic. Many contemporary rods run fenders simply because the owner desires to have a "restored" car. One of the great things about building a hot rod is that you can build your hot rod as you desire. Being safe, within your budget, and in good taste are the only real requirements.

Being safe requires using high quality parts that have been proven to be reliable when used correctly. Being within your budget is between you and your significant other, whether that is a spouse or your banker. Being in good taste is purely subjective. There are no written laws or secret codes that determine "good taste"; however, it is sometimes apparent that there should be. The great thing about building a hot rod is that you can express your individuality and creativity. Like any artist will tell you, though, some people will not share your views. So although you are more than welcome (and encouraged) to be creative, you *may* need to grow some thick skin, at least until your way of thinking catches on with the masses. At most any rod event or gathering where you may find a hot rod, there will always be at least one hot rod that isn't as widely accepted as the rest.

BODY MATERIAL

Throughout the buildup of your hot rod, you will no doubt end up working with a variety of materials. Whether a hot rod is based on an original body or a reproduction thereof, it will likely end up with at least a little bit of both in the final product.

Gennie steel

If you are beginning your hot rod with an original (i.e., genuine or "gennie") steel body, you will undoubtedly have some rust to deal with. It may be minor, or it may be major, but it will be present in at least a minimal amount. When searching for a body, don't let some surface rust scare you away from an otherwise solid car. Even if the entire car is covered with true surface rust, you can deal with it quite easily. Whether you get down to bare metal by hand sanding, a chemical stripper, or media blasting, you won't have a major problem with surface rust.

If the rust goes all the way through a panel or has heavily pitted the metal, you should do some research before you spring the long green for that "gennie" body. Is a replacement "patch" panel available, or could you easily (affordably) make one? If the rusty metal is in a removable panel, such as a fender or a hood, is a replacement available for the vehicle in question?

Another thing you must investigate when dealing with rust is the amount of hidden damage. This can be an eye-opener whether you are considering an abandoned vehicle sitting in a field or barn or a vehicle that someone else has "already done all the hard work" on. A relatively small (perhaps easily repairable) rust hole in a cowl or firewall may have allowed rain, mud, and who knows what else to damage a body mount or inner door hinge support. If the vehicle in question is a driver or other fully-assembled car, the current owners may not have known about the hidden damage when they did their rebuild—but then again, maybe they did and chose to ignore it.

Reproduction

Your hot rod project search may well lead you to a reproduction body. There is a wide variety from which to choose, with more to come in the future. Fiberglass bodies are the most common and offer the widest variety. A limited number of steel bodies are available from a few different companies. For the ultimate in custom, you can contact your local coach builder for a one-off steel body; however, you can expect to pay a bundle to go that route. Bodies made from composite materials are beginning to become available, but it may be too soon to determine their popularity or chances for growth.

If you are looking for something a bit different, you may be required to hot rod an original steel car. Try to obtain all of the trim pieces when you purchase the vehicle, as repro pieces may be difficult to find.

Although it has some ventilation holes around the lower portion of the body, this Model A Tudor body seems fairly solid. Any necessary patch panels are readily available, so this Model A could be the start of a great project.

Brookville Roadsters can sell you a complete chassis and body package if you are looking for a steel Model A or 1932 Ford roadster. Brookville Roadsters

Steel Ford roadster bodies are currently available in steel reproduction for the 1928 through 1932 model years, along with roadster pickups for the Model A years (1928-1931), from Brookville Roadsters. The 1932 Ford roadster body is also being reproduced by Rod Bods, with minor differences between the two bodies. Steel roadster bodies are also available from Steve's Auto Restorations if a 1933 or 1934 is more to your liking.

The price differences between a steel repro and a high-quality fiberglass repro body may be negligible. Accurately considering factors such as delivery time, amount of prep work prior to paint, and the personal desire (or lack thereof) to build/own a steel car will be your best guides in deciding between steel and fiberglass.

Fiberglass Fiberglass can be good and it can be bad. For one thing, fiberglass will not rust, period. If you live in a climate where road salt or salt from the sea are common, or you just aren't too good about keeping your hot rod clean, a fiberglass car may be the best thing for you.

On the other hand, fiberglass can crack or warp. For the most part, however, proper curing and paint preparation/application will avoid these pitfalls. Giving the body enough time to fully cure and avoiding applying dark color paint are the two main keys to getting the most out of a fiberglass body. Sanding a fiberglass body all over with 80-grit sandpaper and letting it sit in the summer sun as much as possible will help the body to cure fully.

CONCEPT

If you are contemplating building a hot rod, you should first decide what you want the outcome to be and then determine how to get there. It's a choice you'll want to make carefully, because once you're done, your completed rod may not match the vision of any prospective buyers—

A newcomer on the scene is Hot Rods and Horsepower, builder of a steel 1932 Ford coupe body. Hot Rods and Horsepower had this prototype 1934 Ford coupe body on display at the NSRA Street Rod Nationals.

at least not at a price you'd like. Although several people make a living by building hot rods, it is usually done by having a customer commission the construction and then pay for the project as it progresses. To build a hot rod on a speculation basis (while attempting not to go broke or insane) is not a task for the masses.

If you desire to own a hot rod and have the time, the knowledge (or the willingness to learn), and the ability to ride the rod-building roller coaster, you can earn a great feeling of accomplishment from building it yourself.

If you don't have all of those characteristics, you can have a hot rod built for you. There is no shame in paying someone else to do the work. Just remember who is paying

Above: *This is a Show Me Rod & Custom fiberglass body mounted on a Morfab Customs chassis. For best results when using a fiberglass body, it is recommended to scuff the entire body with 80-grit sandpaper and then allow it to sit in the summer sun for as long as possible before doing final block sanding and paint prep. Any fiberglass product needs to cure properly.*
Below: *Many hot rods are never driven, simply because the owner can afford to build a high visibility garage ornament. This writer will always believe that true enjoyment of a hot rod, whether it is home built or professionally built, comes from getting behind the wheel and heading down the highway.*

Although the wood body may require an extra amount of upkeep, this phantom 1932 Ford woodie sure looks sharp. If you have a chassis and a cowl, you can construct your own phantom woodie.

and who is building. The builder you choose becomes your "expert consultant," so you should be able to ask for their technical advice. They should be able to explain the options to you and allow you to make the final decision based on cost, performance, and personal appeal. Likewise, you are the customer. Therefore, leave the construction process to them. The builder will ask you certain questions, giving you some options. You will need to have an answer for them within a reasonable time frame, or your project is going to be pushed into a corner somewhere. Do some asking around and get some references beforehand if you

choose to have someone build a hot rod for you. Making sure you're dealing with a reliable person who has the skills, motivation, and means to do your project can save you a lot of heartache, including unreasonable delays, inept work, or even the loss of your money or project.

Purpose of the vehicle

Whether you are building a hot rod strictly by yourself, paying someone to build it, or a combination of the two, you need to determine the purpose of the vehicle very early in the process. Having everything plated and polished as on a show car may not be practical for a daily driver, while a "right out of the box" carburetor won't win any detailing points at a car show.

Although the running boards are missing in this photo, this primered truck served as a daily driver (and subject of several magazine how-to articles) for the author for two years and over 40,000 miles. It was nothing flashy, but it received its fair share of thumbs-ups between home and the office.

Certainly not a Thom Taylor drawing, but you have to start somewhere. When planning a hot rod project, a drawing or photograph will help to maintain direction toward your final goal.

Another nostalgic rod is this 1940 Ford coupe. Note the bright yellow paint, painted steelies with hubcaps and trim rings, and wide whitewall tires.

Show car Hot rods being built strictly for the show circuit are not as common as they once were. Oh, sure, there are still a lot of shows or "judged events" to compete in, and the number of rods being entered continues to grow. The contemporary school of thought seems to be to build a hot rod toward winning shows, make the show circuit for a year, and then put the hot rod on the street.

To win (or even compete) in these big shows is no small task. To capture the America's Most Beautiful Roadster award or the Ridler Award, takes hundreds of thousands of dollars.

A predecessor to the more common T-bucket is this early hot rod Model T roadster. Although this one is all new, it is period perfect with the quick-change rear, wide whites, engine dress-up, and coon tail hanging from the mirror. Gary Moore

This includes parts, construction, detailing, cleaning, and transportation. For the most part, simply bolting on an aftermarket polished billet widget is not going to be enough. You will need to detail that part somehow to make it different from the one on the show promoter's daily driver. Construction will need to be very precise, careful, and consistent. "Good enough" just isn't if you are serious about competing in the major hot rod shows of today. Yes, the judges will see that. Gaps between body panels must be consistent with no ifs, ands, or buts. Detailing can include everything from routing wires a certain way, to having the heads of all the screws turned the same way. Anything you can think of to approach perfection is necessary if you want to win a big show. Extensive cleaning and transportation in an enclosed trailer or truck will be the easiest portion of winning.

There have been occasions, both past and present, when many show-only cars didn't really even run. Nothing says that you can't chrome an entire engine block. Perhaps even mill a block out of stainless steel if it won't be required to run. No need to install pistons or a crankshaft either.

Weekend hot rod Many of these one-time show cars and most other hot rods are built to be weekend hot rods. That is not meant to say that you can't drive one to the grocery store or a cruise night through the week. What it does mean is that most rods are built for pleasure. Whether you attend a rod run somewhere every weekend, drive on a month-long vacation, or just cruise around town, a weekend hot rod is not your only transportation.

How often, when, where, and how long you plan to drive your hot rod are important questions that deserve

Two-tone paint jobs can look great if the colors complement each other. A pinstripe or subtle graphic is needed to tie the two colors together.

honest answers. Reliability is important if you plan to drive it at all, but we will discuss that more a bit later. How often you plan to drive may give you some insight as to practicality. If you plan to do a lot of driving, you may not want a 1000-horsepower engine that consumes a gallon of fuel between the garage and the end of the driveway. If you are going to be traveling great distances to rod runs or vacation destinations that are extremely hot, you may want a closed car so you can have effective air conditioning. If you live in a mild climate, an open car may be cool enough. How long are you going to be driving? Make it comfortable for more than that.

Daily driver For any vehicle that you intend to use as a daily driver, your emphasis has to be on reliability, serviceability, practicality, comfort, and safety. With proper maintenance, a well-built hot rod should be just as reliable as any factory-built vehicle. On occasion, it may be necessary to charge the battery or change a flat tire. How difficult is it to get to the battery? How hard would it be to get one of those pro-street tires from inside the fender if you have a flat in the middle of nowhere? Did you ever have to change one of those in-the-fuel-tank fuel pumps alongside the road?

A daily driver is not the place to be exotic, but that doesn't mean you can't be cool. Proper planning, use of relatively easy-to-replace parts, and some common sense will pay off if you're going to drive your hot rod every day.

Style

Style, concept, or whatever you choose to call it is without a doubt one of the most important considerations before you

purchase a single part for your hot rod. You need to have at least a visual idea in your mind of how you want the finished product to look before you shop for parts. Whether that vision is a car you saw on the cover of *HOT ROD* magazine, one that old guy who worked at the body shop owned, or a combination of ideas, you need to be able to see it in your mind. If you can draw it or have someone else do that for you, it will help you see the light through the Bondo dust. It is not just by coincidence that many famous, award-winning hot rods are based on drawings by such guys as Thom Taylor, Chip Foose, Steve Stanford, and David Thacker.

Like too many cooks spoiling the stew, incorporating too many different styling ideas in one vehicle may yield a less than desirable outcome. Although it could be done, you probably wouldn't want to use bias ply tires with large diameter billet wheels. Likewise, you probably wouldn't want to use cowl lights on a chopped-top, smoothed, monochromatic 1948 Chevrolet fastback. Or a classic Tijuana tuck-and-roll interior on a high-dollar, contemporary, over-the-top show rod.

Traditional To build a "true" traditional hot rod, such as one geared toward the forties or fifties era, you would need to scour a lot of salvage yards and swap meets, along with being a subscriber to *Hemmings Motor News* to find all of the necessary parts. On this traditional rod, you may need to forego things that we take for granted, such as an alternator, tilt wheel, radial tires, and disc brakes. Most people are not going to harass you for having radial tires or disc brakes since those are serious safety-related items. However, a rod using a Ford flathead block with Offy heads, beehive oil

Looking much like a Dave Bell drawing, this 1932 Ford coupe features many modifications that go unnoticed by the causal observer. Getting the right stance, ride height, and attitude takes a careful eye.

filter, and transparent red fuel lines just loses a bit of credibility when it sits on 20-inch billet wheels.

If you build your hot rod like one created in the sixties or seventies, you can justifiably use equipment that is more common. A small block Chevy engine would be appropriate, but then again, so would a Cadillac, Buick, or Oldsmobile engine. Can't forget blown Chrysler hemi engines, either.

As rodders evolve, we are finding more ways to make equipment appear old timey yet still function more efficiently. Disc brake kits can now be easily made to look like finned Buick drum brakes, while more late engines are being adapted to accept early valve covers. The stuff you use doesn't have to be old if you can make it look that way.

Contemporary As the twentieth century wound down, hot rods really experienced an evolution in styling. The general plan was to get rid of anything that didn't look like it belonged on a hot rod. Eliminate anything that would make a ripple if the hot rod in question was in a wind tunnel. Remove the cowl lights, smooth the door handles, hide the door hinges, and make this thing smooth. Although it was done with more finesse during this time period perhaps, isn't this basically what rodders at the dry lakes were doing in the forties and fifties? More proof that what goes around comes around.

Perhaps we have now come full circle, as any style can be popular as long as you do it tastefully. Whether you build a supersmooth, monochromatic, slammed-on-the-ground coupe or sedan, or a buggy-sprung, highboy roadster with no hood, it can be well received. Use some

common sense, determine what components work well together, avoid the ones that don't, and you can have a neat hot rod. Just remember that guys and gals have been building hot rods for a long time. If you think of something that you haven't seen before, you might want to mention it to your friends before you build it. There may be a reason some of those ideas never saw the light of day, or any magazine coverage.

State-of-the-art If you think you want to build a hot rod that will make everything else pale in comparison, you had better be in your banker's good graces. If you really want to make a statement, there is no room to cut corners. Each component along with each phase of the construction must be at the same level of perfection. If you have the ability to purchase or make all of the parts, can assemble them correctly, and can disassemble, paint, polish, and reassemble all of them, you may get away without an outrageous labor bill. However, the time spent will quickly add up.

This is certainly not an effort to deter anyone from building a state-of-the-art hot rod. Several are built each year, and many win awards and grace the covers of magazines. If that is your sole intention for building a hot rod, so be it. Realize that even if your hot rod is on the cover of every rod magazine published, that cover will be outdated within a month.

THE PLAN

Once you have a vision of the hot rod you'd like to build, you need a clear plan of how to make it a reality—before money starts pouring out of your wallet. Without a clear plan from the beginning, you'll end up spending more time and money before the project is finally finished . . . or abandoned. Whether you are doing the work yourself or contracting it out, having to redo something is never a good thing. If any of your parts don't work together, you'll need to purchase or fabricate different parts. Even if the hot rod parts store is next door, the new part will cost something. Making it yourself will at least take some time.

This is not to say that you shouldn't redo something if necessary. If a certain part of your hot rod's construction appears to be faulty or unsafe, whether through lack of knowledge, lack of caring, or something that just didn't work as designed, go ahead and redo whatever needs to be done. It is much wiser to delay completion of a project slightly by fixing something when you first notice it than to finish the entire car only to discover that you can't fix the problem without a lot of disassembly. Learn to work smarter, not harder.

Who is going to do the work?

Much like planning "what" you want to build, "who" will do the work requires some thought as well. More than likely, for various reasons, you are not going to be able to complete your hot rod without at least some help. If you can build the strongest engine around, you may feel uncomfortable when it comes to upholstery work. Even if you are good with a spray gun and primer and are able to do bodywork and paint prep, you may not have the proper facilities or patience to actually spray the top color coats of paint. Any of a number of things will keep you from single-handedly building a hot rod from start to finish. Deciding up front what you can likely take on and what you'll want to contract out will help you budget your time and expenses.

What can you do yourself? If you are a novice to the rod building world, you may think you can't do any of the work. You owe it to yourself, however, to at least try. With that in mind, what are the logical things you can do? You may be able to straighten a dented fender, or you may hammer it into oblivion. Other than the need to replace said fender, what have you lost? You may be out some time, but your time is cheap. Everyone else's, on the other hand, is expensive. If you can learn to hammer out small dents, you can then learn how to mix up and sling some body filler over the depression and sand it to make it smooth. If you can do this much, mixing some primer and spraying it on the necessary area isn't too big a deal. If you break the big job into smaller tasks, it will seem easier. In this

scenario, the worst thing to happen is that your hot rod has a wavy fender. In the big scheme of things, that's not so bad. Depending on your ability and results, that professional body man's estimate may not seem so outrageous on your next project.

What else can you do? Since you are the person who will be driving the car, and therefore troubleshooting it, it would make sense for you to wire it yourself. Wiring should not be taken lightly (and cannot be done by just anyone); however, a little complexity should not keep you from taking on this responsibility. If you are familiar with basic electronic principles and the components used in your hot rod, you can wire it from scratch if you choose. With the large number of wiring kits currently available, using a prefabricated fuse panel and appropriate wiring, this once daunting task can now be somewhat enjoyable. With the intimate knowledge of your hot rod that you will gain by wiring it yourself, you will be better equipped to handle an electrical problem while on the road. Other than trial by fire, you can't do too much damage by wiring the car yourself. Following the instructions and using common sense will keep you from burning your hot rod to the ground.

However, if you do not feel comfortable doing the wiring, hire someone you trust to do it for you. A wiring snafu that leaves you alongside the road waiting for a tow truck instead of drinking a glass of lemonade with your buddies at a rod run, is no fun.

Upholstery is something that can be learned (if you have the right mindset for it) and will not hurt anyone if not done correctly. You may get your feelings hurt if someone comments that your stitches aren't straight or points out your lack of color-coordination skills when you debut your purple coupe with lime green corduroy interior. Other than that, lack of experience on your part is not going to hurt an innocent bystander.

What should be subcontracted? Anything that you have tried and just can't do adequately or anything that you don't feel you can do safely should be subcontracted. Most any rodder's garage now includes a MIG welder. For welding in a patch to repair a door or quarter panel, a MIG welder lets just about anyone produce a satisfactory weld (although the amount of body filler and sanding required to finish the panel may vary). That same rodder who seems to do a decent job on sheet metal may not have the knowledge, experience, or equipment to weld in a frame crossmember. The welding theory may be the same, but the crossmember to which the front suspension is mounted is a bit more critical to your safety than any patch panel.

If you don't have access to a well-lit, very clean, extremely well-ventilated area, you should probably pass on doing the paint work on your hot rod. The paint is one of the things that stands out most on any hot rod, so it is natural to want to do it yourself. Being able to position parts so that you can easily see and access them to provide full coverage is not always as easy as it sounds. Keeping the dust and dirt out of the fresh paint is also a potential problem.

With ever-tightening regulations, not having the proper facility is one of the main reasons that more rods are not painted at home. Allowing paint fumes to collect in your neighbor's airspace is not a great way to gain their acceptance of your hot rod. Your own health and well-being are also of primary concern, as the harmful effects of paint products are not only inhaled but also soaked up through your skin and your eyes. Therefore, a paint suit and full face mask are essential.

What parts to use?

With all of the reproduction parts available, many people have the false notion that all a person has to do to build a hot rod is to bolt a bunch of parts together. Ask anyone who has built a hot rod and he or she will tell you that is not the case. Having the new parts available and delivered to your garage door may be easier than scrounging through a salvage yard for that certain part, but there is also a downside.

Just because a repro part says that it's for a 1938 Whatzit doesn't mean that it won't have to be modified to fit correctly. We have to remember that many of the parts we order from catalogs are reproductions of original parts. If the original (from which the mold or pattern was made) was damaged, modified, or just plain didn't fit right from the factory, how can we expect the reproduction of that piece to fit correctly? Depending on the process used when making the new pieces, the mold or pattern may also start to show some signs of wear or misalignment problems.

Some parts used on hot rods are not reproductions but simply new parts made to do an old job and look good at the same time. Many companies have made great strides toward making these parts user friendly; however, some are better designed than others. Some of these pieces will work great after you figure out how to install them, but you had better hope that you never actually have to service or otherwise remove that part from your hot rod. Before you spend your hard-earned money, ask some other hot rodders if their installations of the latest widget went okay. Ask if they have any recommendations on how to do it differently if they were to do it again. Building a hot rod is supposed to be fun, so don't be too shy to ask some questions if it will make your project go easier.

It is also necessary to learn which parts work well together and which ones don't. For instance, a small block Chevrolet engine can have a short water pump or a long water pump. If space is not a concern, either one will work fine. However, in most pre-1948 hot rods, it will be necessary to use the short water pump if you plan to keep the radiator and grille shell in the stock location. Don't be afraid to read the fine print and all of the footnotes when you are looking through all of those parts catalogs.

What are they going to cost? Quite simply . . . a bunch. Finished hot rods have a wide variety of price tags on them. Part of the reason for this is that no one remembers to add up *everything* that went into its construction. The price variation doesn't come from what is included as much as from what was left out. Obviously, you have the cost of the parts themselves. What about shipping? Someone has to pay the guys and gals in the big brown trucks to deliver these parts to your door. Even if you purchase the parts locally, you probably didn't walk to the parts store! Unless all of your parts are chromed or polished stainless, they will need to be painted. This simple process quickly adds primer, body filler, masking tape, sandpaper, and paint. Whether you add all of this stuff into the building cost of your hot rod while asking your banker or spouse for a loan is up to you, but the costs will be there regardless. Like it or not, a finished hot rod can usually be purchased for less money than buying all of the unassembled, unpainted parts separately.

Now that you have the cost and related expenses of the parts calculated, you need to consider your time. If you are building a hot rod because you want to build a hot rod, your time is free. We all need a sanity project, and building a hot rod can be a good one. If you are building a hot rod because you think selling the completed car will turn a quick buck, you should rethink your plan.

For a rough look at the cost of building a hot rod, refer to the following table. This is based on current prices for components chosen to build a fenderless 1932 Ford roadster pickup. This "project" vehicle would not have fenders or running boards, thereby eliminating some expense. It also would not include air conditioning or a stereo. By eliminating some chrome, the cost could be brought down some more. However, adding any of the above would obviously raise the price. Although the prices are current as this is written, this is by no means an all-inclusive list of *all* the parts necessary for building this particular hot rod.

When should I order the parts? In a perfect world, you could order all of the parts you need at one time. Then you could simply bolt them together and your hot rod would be finished in no time. In reality, however, being able to do that would be a rare case.

Most of the parts used in building a hot rod will be required to interact with various other parts when the vehicle is completed. Obviously, you need fifteen-inch

TABLE 3

1932 FORD HIGHBOY ROADSTER PICKUP PROJECT

Component	MSRP
Rolling chassis components:	
1932 Ford reproduction frame	$6,298.00
Complete 4-bar front suspension	Included
Front 4-bar, chrome	Included
4-inch dropped I-beam axle	Included
Adjustable front spring perches	Included
Spring shackles	Included
Front spring	Included
Front spring plate and U-bolts	Included
Front spring clamps	Included
Front shocks, chrome	Included
'37–'41 Ford spindles	Included
Tie rod arms	Included
Spindle/hub nuts and washers	Included
Standard kingpin set	Included
Steering component kit, pitman arm, and tie rod	Included
Front Panhard kit	Included
Spindle stop nuts	Included
Nine-inch Ford rear end housing and axles	Included
Nine-inch Ford third member, 3.70:1 gears, 28 spline, open differential	Included
Rear 4-bar, chrome	Included
Rear coilover shocks	Included
Rear Panhard kit	Included
Front disc brakes	Included
Rear drum brakes	Included
C-notch frame for rear axle clearance	$85.00
Pinch frame rails and notch front cross member	$125.00
Chrome front-end options	$450.00
Wheels, 15 x 5 front	$110.00
Wheels, 15 x 8.5 rear	$130.00
Tires, 145 x 15 front	$175.00
Tires, P285/70R15 rear	$200.00
Lug nuts	$30.00
Hubcaps	$114.00
Rolling chassis components subtotal	***$7,717.00***
Body components:	
1932 Ford Roadster pickup body	$3,390.00
Bed sheet metal	$1,550.00
Three-piece hood w/louvered sides	$350.00
Duval windshield	$995.00
Grille shell	$590.00
Gas tank (universal)	$219.00
Front spreader bar w/integral turn signals	$225.00
Front license plate brackets	$52.00
Headlights	$55.47
Hi-boy headlight brackets	$58.00
Braided stainless steel headlight conduits	$54.95
Taillights	$50.00
Third taillight	$89.95
Glass, tinted	$400.00
Body components subtotal	***$8,079.37***
Drivetrain components:	
330-horsepower, 350-cubic-inch GM engine	$3,095.99
GM 200 4R automatic transmission w/overdrive	$1,200.00

Electric fan	$145.95
Transmission oil cooler	$30.00
Speedometer cable	$51.95
Aluminum driveshaft	$300.00
Radiator	$675.00
Radiator cap	$19.95
Radiator recovery tank	$75.00
Headers	$525.00
Starter	$125.00
Alternator	$100.00
Alternator bracket	$80.00
Crankshaft pulley	$64.95
Water pump pulley	$74.95
Air cleaner	$25.00
Thermostat housing	$25.00
Steering box	$329.00
Steering shafts and U-joints	$225.00
Drivetrain components subtotal	***$7,167.74***

Brake system components:

Dual master cylinder	Included w/chassis price
32 Ford brake pedal	Included w/chassis price
Thru frame fittings	$39.95
Front stainless brake lines	$57.63
Rear stainless brake lines	$57.63
Proportioning valve	$59.95
Residual valve 2#	$25.75
Residual valve 10#	$25.75
³⁄₁₆-inch brake line	$35.00
Brake system components subtotal	***$301.66***

Interior components:

Steering column	$275.00
Steering column drop	$50.00
Steering wheel	$125.00
Steering column floor trim	$32.95
Gauges	$280.00
Dash indicator lights	$12.00
Bench seat	$800.00
Throttle pedal	$58.66
Transmission shifter and linkage	$220.00
Three-point seat belts	$180.00
Emergency brake lever and linkage	$160.00
Wiring panel and kit	$275.00
Throttle cable	$33.39
Kick-down cable	$51.87
Brake pedal pad	$30.00
Interior components subtotal	***$2,583.87***
Parts Subtotal	***$25,849.64***

Labor and materials:

Powder coating (chassis and components)	$1,000.00
Paint and related products	$5,000.00
Upholstery (top, seat, and interior)	$3,500.00
Labor and materials subtotal	***$9,500.00***
APPROXIMATE BUILD AND FINISH PRICE	**$35,349.64**

Buying all of your parts from one source and at one time is a great way to build a hot rod if you can afford to do that. This roadster pickup from Brookville Roadsters would be easy enough to finish in a relatively short time. Add a drivetrain, wiring, plumbing, upholstery, and paint, and you're done. Brookville Roadsters

wheels if you are going to run fifteen-inch tires. What isn't so obvious (and very critical if building a fendered car) is what offset the wheels should have. It is perhaps easiest to have the desired wheels and tires mounted and then to purchase a rear end that is the correct width to keep that wheel and tire combination tucked inside the fenders. Of course, to do that, you need to have the fenders. Depending on what make and model of car you are building, properly locating the fenders may require that you have the running boards as well. See how this quickly becomes a domino effect?

What this all boils down to is preliminary planning. When you see a hot rod that you like, ask the owner what he or she did to make it look like that. Most rodders will be glad to tell you more than enough about their pride and joy. After you decide what make and model of hot rod you want to build, look at every other one of the same type that you can. See what looks good and what doesn't. When you determine such things as what wheel and tire combination looks best, determine what other components will be affected by their sizes. Low and wide pro-street tires are going to require a narrower rear end than a taller, skinnier sport truck radial tire.

As you determine other specific parts that you want to use, figure out what additional parts will be affected by your choices. Acquire the ones that are limited as far as size, finish, etc., and then determine what options this leaves you for the other parts.

When do you need to do what?

When building a hot rod, it is best to plan whether you are going to finish the car completely before you drive it or build a work in progress. Life can throw you some unexpected curves at times, and it is not all bad (and very common) if

your project gets delayed somewhere along the line.

If you plan to build your car in stages, you will perhaps be able to enjoy it sooner. The drawback is that you may spend more time in the actual building process this way, but you would not be the first person to go this route. A typical scenario is to get the chassis work completed, drop in a junkyard motor, do enough wiring to get the engine to run and the lights to work, and you are off to the rod run. After attending your favorite rod runs in the summer, you can concentrate on bodywork and engine detailing over the winter. Another season of rod runs in perhaps one color of primer, and paint and upholstery can be completed in the winter. For many people (whether by choice or otherwise), this method of rod building works well. Getting your hot rod out on the road is the one sure way to verify that everything works as planned and to eliminate the bugs before it is necessary to repair paint and upholstery to do so.

Building your hot rod from start to finish also sounds like a great way to go. If you do it properly, it can be. Breaking in your engine on a test stand, taking the time and effort to remove the body from the car, and reinstalling it at least five or six times are all important if you want to build your car one time and be finished with it. The key to this method is taking the time to do it right so that you don't have to do it over. Yet choosing to do it over in the construction process is better than being required to do so after the car is finished.

The basic steps The basic steps in building a hot rod are to build the chassis, install the drivetrain, mount the body onto the chassis, determine what needs to be done to fit all of the components into the space allowed, make a complete mock-up of everything, disassemble the components, do detailing work, and then assemble the hot rod a final time.

Whether the process takes 12 months or 12 years, to properly build a hot rod, you will have to do all of these steps. Realize that from the beginning and you will be ahead of the game.

When building the chassis, you will need the frame, the suspension components, and the steering components (from the steering box to the wheels). Having the correct wheels and tires (or at least comparable in size to the intended ones) will help you build in the correct amount of caster when installing the front suspension. You'll need the engine and transmission (or a mock-up block and case) to locate the motor and transmission mounts accurately, as well as to mount the rear suspension. Having correct steering geometry and driveline angles will greatly improve your rod building (and driving!) experience.

Whether you do it before or after the body is on the frame, the actual engine and transmission should be installed to determine fan/radiator clearance, exhaust/steering linkage clearance, and engine/firewall clearance.

It will be necessary to have the body and fenders installed prior to measuring for a driveshaft to verify that the wheelbase is correct. The wheels should be centered in the wheel openings; thus, their location determines the driveshaft length—don't move the wheels out of their correct location to suit an improper-length driveshaft. With the body and seats in place, the correct locations for the steering wheel, shifter, gas and brake pedal, and other controls can be determined. You will also need to determine where to install the a/c system, stereo, gas tank, and battery.

Before you paint or polish anything, you want to test-assemble as much of the car as possible. This will allow you to see what fits, what hits, and what just plain won't work. While you are in this mock-up stage, keep in mind that you may be required to service this vehicle sometime, and plan access to those serviceable components.

Ahead of the game or ahead of yourself? By the time you have built a hot rod that will easily fit into a parking space that is less than 175 square feet, you will no doubt have had parts all over the garage, the basement, the attic, and all through the house. While you are strolling through a rod run full of finished hot rods, you will find it hard to believe how much dust, dirt, grease, grime, and absolute filth their construction will produce.

So while you are building the chassis, there is no real need to have the air conditioning unit, the window glass, and the upholstery material in your way. You don't need to have grinding dust settle into that new a/c evaporator, or welding sparks pitting that new tinted glass. If you have the room to store those parts somewhere out of your way, that's fine; but if you are limited to just the garage for your storage and building, you should refrain from ordering parts until you really need them to plan your construction properly. Tripping over a driveshaft and then dropping a cylinder head onto your new radiator while you are looking for your floor jack is not conducive to enjoyable rod building.

Where is the work going to be done?

Obviously, most of the work on a hot rod will be done in a garage or carport. Making sure that you have plenty of light, electrical outlets, and moderate temperature will make your rod building experience more enjoyable. Reasonably secure storage, running water (for cleanup), and telephone access (for calling the parts store or pizza delivery) will also be beneficial. Realize that you will never have too much available space.

Building a hot rod in your own garage Whether you are working in a garage that is attached to your home, a detached garage, or a garage across town, the fact that it is your own is a plus. Throughout the process of building a hot rod, you are rarely going to be able to completely finish any one task in any one work session. If you are fortunate enough to be able to leave your tools and parts sitting where you are using them, instead of being required to put everything away before calling it a day, you will ultimately save some time.

Building a hot rod in someone else's garage On the other hand, if you are working on a hot rod in someone else's garage (tech school, employer's shop after work, or your buddy's garage), other people may need the tools or space you are using. To keep everything in harmony, you will need to do your part to keep your tools and parts properly stowed while not in use.

Building a hot rod in your car club garage Like working in someone else's garage, you will need to keep track of where *your* tools and parts are and where the *club's* tools and equipment are. Being able to share resources is one of the things that makes hot rodding fun, so do your part to keep it that way.

How are you going to pay for this project?

Building a hot rod can be expensive, so you need to have an idea of how you are going to pay for it before you get started. Ideally, you'll have cash in hand when you buy all of the parts and can pay for or trade labor for any work that you have someone else do. Realistically, you may have to stretch out the parts buying over a period of time (as you can afford it), unless you use your fantastic plastic. Beware of that route, as the charge card payment will be due long before the hot rod is completed.

How much is it going to cost to get started? It won't take much to get started in building a hot rod. By buying this book, you have taken one of your first steps. And you can do a lot of additional planning and research at virtually no cost. Beyond that, you can get started for a few hundred dollars—for example, picking up an engine core you can start tearing down for a rebuild; or a few thousand—by buying a suitable hulk to form the basis of your rod (for the most desirable cars this can be many thousand). Just remember to gather as much information as you can before you part with your money to ensure that the parts you acquire will fit and function according to your needs.

How much more will it take to finish? You know most of the parts a functioning car requires. You also know what custom parts you want on your special rod. With that information and whatever parts you've already acquired in hand, you can perform a rough estimate of remaining costs. Get some current parts catalogs and make as complete a list as possible of everything you'll require, including shipping. If you'll need additional tools, list them and look up their cost. Add some representative costs you've gathered from fellow rodders for engine building, paint, and upholstery work, for example, and you'll have a decent ballpark figure. Now add several thousand more for the unforeseen parts and fabrication costs that invariably pop up. It won't be an exact figure, but it will help you determine whether your time frame fits your budget. If not, you may want to scale back your goodies, do more work yourself, or take more time to build it.

A PILE OF JUNK OR A STACK OF PARTS?

Sometime when you are having the inevitable troubles making something work as designed, waiting for a necessary part, or dealing with the financier on your case, you may get discouraged. At these times, all of these parts may just start looking like a pile of junk rather than the components necessary to build the hot rod of your dreams. This will happen. You cannot let it get the best of you, however. At times like these, it is perhaps best to quit working on your hot rod, spend some time with loved ones, and just get away from the project for a while. When you do get back to it, it will go smoother because you will have a new perspective and a new dose of ambition. A good approach, if you feel overwhelmed, is to break the project down into small components. Pick a suitable one, focus only on it, get it done right, and move on—one step at a time, one day at a time.

Starting with repro parts
New parts equals new money The ability to purchase new parts is what has kept hot rodding alive throughout the years. If we had to rely on salvage yards and swap meets, many of today's rodders would be building model railroads or collecting postage stamps instead.

However, new parts are just that and therefore come with new prices. If you can find the component that will fill your needs at a swap meet, you can be assured that it will cost you less than buying the same part new. You just have to be on the lookout for hidden damage or modifications that add repair or replacement costs.

Assembly vs. repair If you are using all new parts, the entire project should go together much more smoothly than if using "veteran" parts. No rust, no grease, and no road grime make it easier to weld or bolt the parts together. This will also keep the entire operation—you, other parts, your work space—cleaner.

If you are starting with an existing vehicle, you will likely need to eliminate existing paint buildup and surface rust before you can even bolt a part on properly. Paint chips, surface rust, and grinder dust can be difficult to remove completely from a vehicle. Of course, you will be required to make a repair to a subassembly on occasion before you can use it.

Starting with an original car
Building a hot rod version of a particular make or model that isn't being reproduced will require you to look for an original version of this car to build. There is nothing wrong with this, and it is what gives hot rodding its diversity.

If you start with something that is a bit "different" from the norm, it may require more passion on your part. Depending on how different your new project is, parts availability and experienced assistance may become hard to find. For this reason, the more complete your unusual choice is when you buy it, the easier it will be to build—even if you can't reuse or modify some of the parts, you'll at least have them on hand as models for their replacements.

Marching to a different drummer sometimes leaves you marching by yourself. That said, don't be afraid to think outside the box. Many hot rods are based on vehicles that weren't even considered hot rod material a few short years ago. Until Fat Jack Robinson landed his '46 Ford on the cover of *HOT ROD* magazine, few people considered fat Fords as mainstream hot rod material.

Bigger first step suggests "more for your money" During your search you may find a complete or nearly complete hot rod project in the classified ads or at a swap meet. If everything is there and the price is less than what you have in your pocket at the time, you might think it is a great deal. It may be, but then again, it may not.

Before you become overrun with emotion at your new find, make another lap around the swap meet and consult with some of your friends. Are the fenders really as good as they look? Were you going to build a fendered car anyway? What about hidden rust or damage? What about those extra parts . . . are they usable, potential swap meet material or extra stuff that you will need to get rid of?

Repair vs. replacement Okay, you decided that your find at the swap meet was indeed a good deal. You spent the money and hauled it all home. You now need to inventory everything that you obtained in the deal. Determine what pieces you will be able to use, what pieces are good but not for this project, and what stuff needs to go in the dumpster. Pieces that are usable for this project can be further separated into "usable as is" and "usable with repair." Do you know how to repair the particular piece? Is it worth the effort? How much of the stuff may be of great interest to restorers, thereby going into the swap meet pile? Many rodders purchase new parts and pieces with proceeds from selling "gennie" parts to restorers.

Redoing someone else's hot rod

Realize that if you purchase someone else's hot rod, it may always be associated with that original owner/builder. Some people have a problem with that, while others don't. How you handle it is up to you. You may choose to add flames or scallops, change wheels and tires, or completely rebuild the entire car. If it's a good deal on a good car and it's what you want, then don't worry about who else may have driven it before you.

Look before you leap When you are contemplating purchasing an existing hot rod, you are certainly entitled to ask some questions. For the price of any hot rod these days, you as the potential buyer are entitled to more than a test drive.

Why is it for sale? If the answer is "Because it rides like an ox cart" or "It burns more oil than gasoline," you may want to pass. But then again, if you have the ability to diagnose a vehicle's problems accurately and are able to remedy them, it may be a great deal. It may be that the current owner is just tired of dealing with something that he or she doesn't have the knowledge or time to fix.

If everything seems as it should with the car, it may be that the owner really enjoys building hot rods more than driving them. This is a very common situation. Maybe the owner just needs to sell to free up capital. Needing to put the kids through school, taking an overdue vacation, making a major home improvement, or simply wanting to do something different as a hobby are all reasons to sell perfectly good hot rods.

Is it worth the price? Pricing anything is difficult, but hot rods can be very difficult. Classified ads show a wide range of prices for different yet similar vehicles. Couple this with the fact that no one really seems to know what those cars should sell for and you can really become confused.

Knowing what similar hot rods are going for will help when negotiating a price. Determine beforehand what you can afford to spend on that hot rod of your dreams. If the vehicle you are checking out is what your dreams are made of and within your budget, it's a done deal. If it's what you want but more pricey than you think it's worth or can afford, feel free to make an offer. The worst thing the owner can do is say no.

Keep in mind that cash talks. If you are serious about buying and have the money (whether you have saved it or you got a loan), actually having the cash with you will inevitably save you some money. The need to be careful when carrying that amount of cash should go without saying. Many hot rods change hands at national events, so having cash can make that perfect hot rod yours if the other interested party has to obtain a cashier's check or apply for a loan.

If the vehicle is close to what you want, but not quite, what will it take to get it the way you want it? Determine what costs will be involved to finish it your way, and deduct this from the asking price. A few sellers may be firm on their price, but if they want to sell, they are usually willing to negotiate.

Making it your car Does it have a clear (legal) title? Before handing over the cash, you should always verify that your next hot rod has a clear title. The last thing you want to do is fork out a bunch of money for something that you can't legally license and drive. Although stolen vehicles are relatively rare among hot rods (compared to Corvettes and other collectible cars), you, for sure, don't want to buy one.

Obtaining a legal title Often, you will find a vehicle (or parts vehicle) that is a good deal but does not have a title. It may be that the owner has died or that the car went to a scrap yard without a title. If you have verified that the vehicle that you want to buy is not stolen, you can buy a new title. Actually, you would be buying an old title. Several companies advertise in various rodding publications for old car titles. Call them and tell them what kind of car you have. If they have a title for the vehicle you want, you send them a check, and they send you a title. Well worth the cost to avoid going through the paperwork of obtaining a licensable title from a salvage title.

CHAPTER 2
CHASSIS

FRAME

The frame for your hot rod is literally the foundation of your rolling masterpiece. No matter how smooth your bodywork is, how fast the engine runs, or how flashy the paint and wheels are, if the chassis is substandard, so is your hot rod. The frame must solidly support the body without any flexing. Suspension components will need to flex, but the frame must remain rigid. If a weak frame allows the body to flex, numerous bodywork problems will quickly develop.

Stock

As this is written, the newest stock hot rod frame is more than fifty years old, while the older frames are quickly approaching eighty. Even if these frames have never been damaged, they require at least some modification to meet today's driving styles and road conditions.

Boxing the frame rails Most original frames are constructed from steel channel. This channel construction is susceptible to damage from side impact, as well as from above or below. One of the most common modifications to strengthen a stock frame is to box the rails. Basically, this is simply welding a piece of plate steel across the open side of the channel, creating a stronger box cross section. Of course, the actual profile of the frame makes this task a bit more difficult than that simple explanation.

The upper and lower flanges of the original frame may not be the same width. If they are not, the wider flange must be trimmed so that the boxing plate and the outer frame rail are parallel when the boxing is completed. Any attempt to box original frame rails that have different-width flanges will prove to be a headache.

Even if the complete frame is not boxed, it should be boxed in the area of the motor mounts and the crossmember.

Replacing the crossmember Replacing the crossmember in a frame can be of multiple benefits. New crossmember are usually welded in place after the frame rails have been boxed. By positioning the front crossmember higher in the frame rails, you will actually lower the front of the vehicle. On an early Ford frame, it is common to place the top of the front crossmember flush with the top of the frame rails. This may only be good for an inch, but it can help obtain that just-right stance.

Likewise, the transmission crossmember can be raised slightly to provide a bit more ground clearance. Care must be taken when determining this location, however, as it could interfere with the body sitting properly on the frame. If the transmission crossmember is too high in the frame, it will interfere with the floorboards. If it is positioned too low in the frame, it will cause ground clearance problems.

This chassis by Pete & Jake's Hot Rod Parts provides a good look at a rolling chassis before a body goes on it. With all brackets welded in place, suspension installed, and brake lines run, this chassis needs little more than a body, drivetrain, and wiring to be movable under its own power.

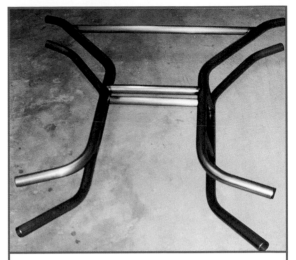

Most original frames (except GM) were constructed of a "C"-shaped channel frame. Front and rear crossmember, and sometimes one in the center, tie the two rails together. Most reproduction chassis are boxed to greatly improve their strength.

This K-member transmission mount greatly improves chassis strength. It is welded to the frame rails in eight places, and it also provides a mount for the transmission tailshaft.

Some transmission crossmember are simply a tube that connects to each frame rail while supporting the tailshaft of the transmission. This type does little to make the frame more rigid. If a K-member or X-member type transmission mount can be employed, it will help to eliminate chassis flex.

The rear crossmember usually serves as a mounting point for coilover shocks. It must be positioned so that it does not bottom out on the rear axle housing or put the coilovers in a bind.

Reproduction

Although good original frames can be found, they are getting scarce. Unless you just happen to have a pristine original in your garage, you are probably time and money ahead purchasing a repro frame from any of a number of manufacturers. Even if you desire to build a purely custom chassis, a set of reproduction frame rails will give you a good place to start. With a sturdy frame jig and excellent welding skills, you can have a custom frame without first having to repair the original "veteran" frame rails.

Most hot rod shops sell their chassis packages in stages. Stage one costs less, but as you can imagine, it includes less. Stage three is usually the complete rolling chassis, short of wheels and tires, so it has a bigger price tag. Most shops are fairly standard in what they include with their packages; however, one shop may list a bare perimeter frame with no brackets as their stage one, while another may start with the brackets already welded on. Make sure you are comparing similar parts lists when shopping for a chassis.

As you are shopping for a chassis, it is a good idea to have the basic concept of the completed hot rod in your mind. It is much better to buy a chassis that is already set up with independent suspension than to decide to retro-fit one later. If you are contemplating building a pro-street rod, your chassis builder will need to know that ahead of time. If you are undecided about fendered or fenderless, that's okay, unless you go ahead and pinch the

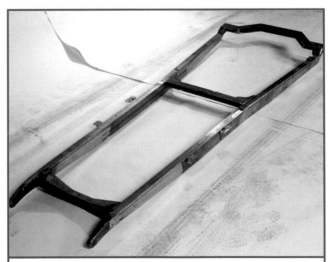

A high-quality reproduction frame will have been built in a jig to assure that it is square and not twisted. This will yield much better results than trying to weld your own chassis on the garage floor. Brookville Roadsters

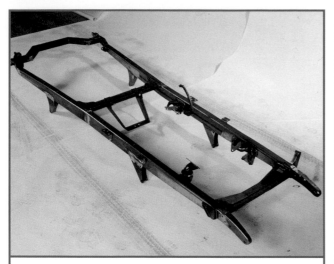

Having the brackets welded on calls for a small bit of commitment. On a four-link suspended rod, you will need to commit to a parallel or triangulated four-link for the rear. Front four-link bars are typically longer on fenderless rods, so you will need to know what you plan to use before the brackets are welded in place. Brookville Roadsters

A four-link suspension handles better than the stock suspension in early rods yet still utilizes the traditional look. Brookville Roadsters

A step closer to having a rolling chassis, this perimeter frame has had all of the brackets welded in place and the suspension components installed. Brookville Roadsters

front frame rails, which will dictate not adding fenders later. Whether your budget requires that you start with a basic frame or allows you to buy a complete chassis, buy from a reputable manufacturer or dealer, as the chassis is the foundation of your hot rod.

Perimeter frame (Stage 1) If you are good with a MIG or TIG welder, using a perimeter frame can be a great way to start your hot rod project. Being nothing more than a straight, square, and clean frame, the cost is minimal. You can mount store-bought or custom-built brackets exactly where you want them to create that one-of-a-kind hot rod.

Perimeter frame plus brackets (Stage 2) If chassis quality welding is not your strong point, but you can operate a combination wrench and a ratchet at the same time, this next chassis package is for you. All of the chassis welding is done, except for some cosmetic bracket boxing that you may choose to have done. Suspension and steering components can be installed later as your budget allows for their purchase. Except for the frame itself, most of the other chassis components can be broken down into three- to five-hundred dollar purchases or less.

Complete chassis (Stage 3) No matter how good a builder you are, if you have the money available and are going to buy repro anyway, buy it all in one fell swoop. This may seem like a lot of money to plunk down at one time; however, most complete chassis sell for less than the sum of the parts if purchased separately.

For the most part, all of the necessary chassis components are included with this package. Some chassis may not include the brakes, brake lines, third member, or rear axles. Again, be sure you are looking at the parts included for the price, not just at the label. If indeed it is a complete chassis, bolt on a set of wheels and tires and you are well on your way to having a hot rod.

Hairpin radius rods locate the front axle in relationship to the frame in the front-to-back direction. Split wishbones or a four-link performs this same task.

Although these components are all reproduction, they utilize the basic original design for the front suspension. The dropped axle and transverse spring are much like the originals; however, the disc brakes are a vast improvement. The four-link helps minimize the bump steer that was common with the stock wishbones suspension. Posies

SUSPENSION

Unlike the frame, the suspension of your hot rod is the part that does flex. The suspension must be able to absorb the vertical motion of the wheels and tires, twisting forces induced by the engine and drivetrain, and horizontal forces such as wind and momentum. Shock absorbers and springs are the main components that control vertical motion. Wishbones, ladder bars, four-links, and radius rods are all components that control the twisting forces. They also work in conjunction with panhard rods and sway bars to limit horizontal forces.

Front

The front suspension obviously suspends the front portion of the hot rod, but it also includes the steering mechanisms. With the concentrated weight of the engine resting on the front suspension, obtaining a smooth ride and easy steering makes correct spring rates and alignment angles mandatory.

Although some people may argue the point, most rodders agree that a 1932 Ford hot rod is going to ride like a stock '32 Ford whether it has a straight axle or an independent front suspension. Until you are driving a postwar car, the ride is thought by many to be about the same in modified or stock

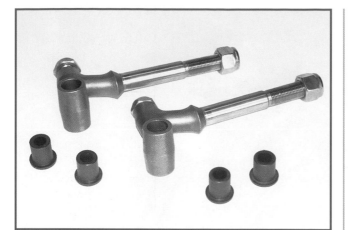

Spring perches perform two tasks on a typical dropped-axle front suspension. The upper part secures one half of the spring shackle. The shaft of the perch passes through a boss in the axle, with the threaded end mounting the lower shock mount. Pete & Jake's Hot Rod Parts

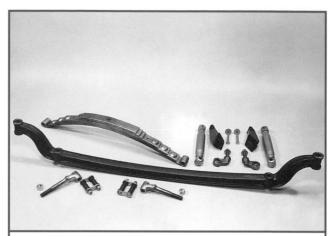

Whether you use a four-link or hairpin radius rods, you will need these items if using a dropped front axle type suspension—front axle, transverse spring, shocks, upper and lower shock mounts, perches, and shackles. Posies

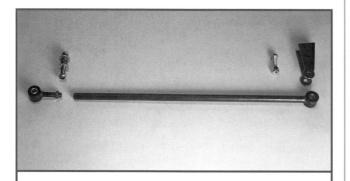

Anytime a transverse spring or coilovers are used, front or rear, a Panhard rod should be used to keep the frame from moving in relationship to the axle. Pete & Jake's Hot Rod Parts

Mustang steering is one way to avoid steering shaft/engine clearance problems. The Mustang steering box exits the vehicle to the side (above, below, or through the frame), then connects to a drag link that is usually mounted outside of the frame rails. (No, I don't know why I didn't think to pick up the trash before I took the picture.)

configuration. Most any thirties-era vehicle is pretty much going to ride the same, whether it has the original suspension a traditional dropped axle with 4-bar or hairpins, or a fully independent suspension. Although a fully polished independent suspension may look trick, it is not going to ride much better than the original suspension. In the larger and heavier vehicles of 1940 vintage and newer, the independent suspension does make a difference in the ride.

Straight axle Most vehicles that we consider hot rod material were originally equipped with a straight front axle. From that beginning, it makes sense that straight axles are still common, although most have been dropped to lower the front of the vehicle. On the older cars, a straight axle (albeit dropped, drilled, and/or filled) just looks natural.

The common setup for a straight axle is for it to be connected to the frame with a set of split wishbones, radius rods, or a four-link. These locate the front axle front to back. At the front of these components, the axle fits into a batwing and is secured in place by the lower end of the spring perch. No matter which of the above locating methods are used, the connection between the axle and the frame rails must be adjustable to allow for obtaining correct caster when aligning the vehicle.

This is a rebuilt 1967–1970 Mustang manual steering box—the standard steering box used with "Mustang" steering in a hot rod. Mullins Steering Gears

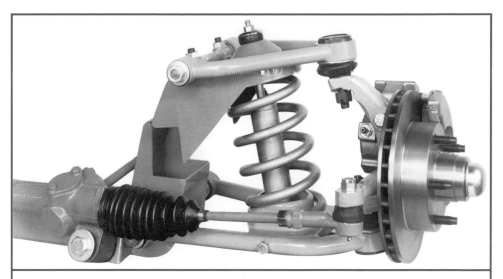

This is a look at an assembled left side of a Mustang II front suspension. Shown are the painted tubular A-arms, spindle with disc brake rotor and caliper, shocks and coil spring, and steering rack. Heidt's Hot Rod Shop

The lower end of the spring perch also serves as an attachment point for the lower shock mount. A transverse leaf spring (multiple leaves or a single leaf) is attached to the top end of the spring perch with a spring shackle. Spring perches may be adjustable to help eliminate binding of the spring. The spring is then secured to the front crossmember by a pair of U-bolts. The upper end of the front shocks are mounted to a shock mount that is welded or bolted onto the top of the frame. Shocks and the spring are what locate the front axle vertically.

Since the spring shackles would allow lateral movement between the axle and the frame, a panhard rod is used to control movement. One end of the panhard rod is mounted to the frame, while the other is mounted to the axle.

A common variation to this straight axle setup is to use coilover (combination shock absorber and coil spring) front shocks instead of separate shocks and leaf spring. The lower end of each coilover is mounted to the axle, while the upper end is mounted to the frame. This eliminates the need for a panhard rod.

Steering in a straight axle hot rod is usually done in one of two ways. One has a steering box (often an early Mustang box, sometimes referred to as "Mustang steering") located near the lower end of the steering column. The Pitman arm (mounted to the steering box) connects the steering arm of the driver's side spindle via a drag link. A tie rod then connects to the opposite side steering arm.

The other common setup is cross-link steering. While this system has been around for a long time, it became more popular in the 1970s with the relatively compact Vega steering box—hence the common name "Vega steering."

The steering column is connected to the steering box (not always a Vega box) via a variety of types of steering shafts. A Pitman arm connects to the steering box; however, it now connects to the passenger side steering arm via a drag link. The passenger side steering arm is then connected to the driver side steering arm via a tie rod.

Independent Aftermarket Mustang II–type independent front suspensions are gaining in popularity as a way to suspend the front of a hot rod. Although they are available for slender-fendered cars, these independent front suspensions are more common on fat-fendered hot rods. Any Mustang II–type front suspension is going to be somewhat bulkier looking than a straight-axle suspension—thus, putting it out of sight under a fat-fendered hot rod is more appropriate.

The typical Mustang II front suspension consists of a weld-in crossmember, two spindles, two upper A-arms, and two lower A-arms. Shock absorbers with coil springs or coilovers are positioned between the outboard end of the lower A-arm and the upper end of the crossmember at the frame rails.

A Mustang II–type front suspension works quite well when installed properly. A large variety of A-arms, from stock to painted tubular and on to polished tubular, makes this suspension appealing no matter what your budget.

Steering for a Mustang II suspension is usually a rack and pinion setup. Both manual and power racks are available; however, the latter is usually not necessary if the suspension is set up properly.

Custom-built independent front suspensions can be

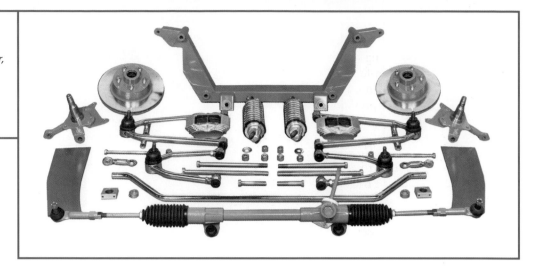

All of the components of a complete Heidt's front suspension—crossmember, boxing plates, spindles, rotors, A-arms, stabilizer bar, and steering rack. Heidt's Hot Rod Shop

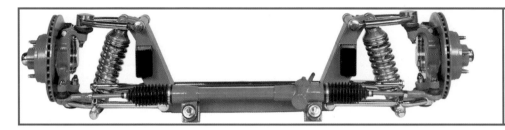

Featuring coilover shocks, this is Heidt's Superide front suspension. Heidt's Hot Rod Shop

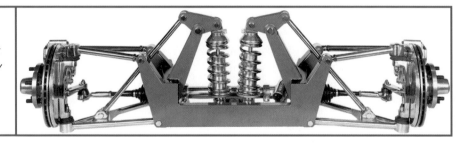

Heidt's open-wheel Superide independent front suspension gives a highboy a sleek appearance. Heidt's Hot Rod Shop

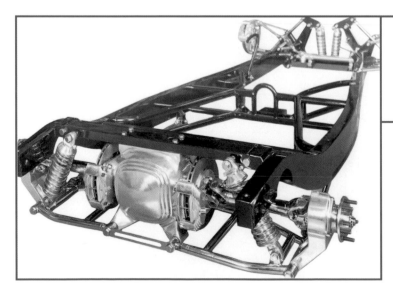

The Heidt's Superide independent rear suspension is shipped assembled, ready for installation on your hot rod. With independent suspension, rear disc brakes, and great looks, this kit is a great value for the money. Heidt's Hot Rod Shop

found under most anything but are more common under slender-fendered or non-fendered hot rods. Utilizing tubular A-arms, rather than bulky-looking stock Mustang II arms, these suspensions provide more of a race car image, as well as a top-notch ride.

Rear

The rear suspension doesn't have to steer, so its mission in addition to suspending the back half of the vehicle is to put the power to the pavement. The rear suspension must locate the rear axle housing front to back and side to side and provide cushion to passengers.

Solid axle The true American hot rod will always be a rear-wheel-drive vehicle. Whether the rearend originally came from Detroit under a four-door sedan, a station wagon, a muscle car, or a pickup truck it doesn't really matter. As long as the housing is the correct width to space the rear wheels and tires between the body and the rear fenders, it doesn't matter what the donor vehicle is. Most any stock-width rear axle housing can be narrowed to fit your particular vehicle.

Leaf springs are a simple and effective way to suspend the rear portion of your hot rod, whether using parallel or transverse springs. Each parallel leaf spring is attached to the frame in front of and behind the rear axle. This locates the axle front to back, as well as side to side, making ladder bars or radius rods unnecessary. The front spring mount is usually in a fixed position, while the rear is allowed to move somewhat via a spring shackle. Solidly mounting both ends

Above: *Heidt's Superide IRS kit has a cast-aluminum alloy center section that includes a Ford 9-inch third member for superior strength.* Heidt's Hot Rod Shop.

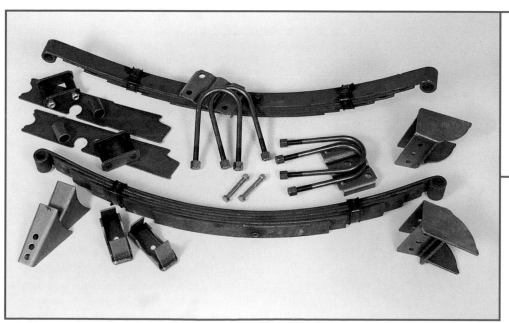

Below: *Posies offers this kit for installing parallel leaf springs on the rear of a 1932 Ford. The kit includes springs, spring hangers, axle mounting pads, boxing plates, shackles, and the necessary hardware.* Posies

of the spring could lead to breakage when encountering uneven pavement or when getting too much traction.

Like the name implies, parallel leaf springs must be kept parallel (when looking down from overhead). The springs may be mounted directly underneath the frame rails, or inboard to allow for additional tire clearance. Parallel leaf springs are secured to the axle with U-bolts and a spring pad.

In their stock configuration, most vehicles that utilize parallel leaves have the springs above the axle. To quickly lower the rear portion of the car the diameter of the rear axle housing, the springs can be run under the axle instead. Placing lowering blocks between the axle and spring pad will lower the vehicle more.

For a more nostalgic rear suspension, you can use a transverse leaf spring. Although it was a stock configuration on many fat-fendered rods, this is typically found beneath earlier body styles now. Each end of the transverse leaf spring is connected to the rear axle with a spring shackle, with the middle of the leaf secured to the rear crossmember. It will be necessary to use radius rods, ladder bars, or a four-link to locate the rear axle housing front to back. The transverse leaf spring will locate the rear axle housing side to side.

Whether you use parallel leaf springs or a transverse spring, you'll also need shock absorbers. The shock's lower end is mounted to the axle, while the upper end is usually mounted to the rear crossmember so that the shock is between 30 and 45 degrees from true vertical.

Although coilovers eliminate leaf springs, they must be used in conjunction with radius rods, ladder bars, or a four-link to locate the rear axle housing front to back. Like shock absorbers, coilovers should be mounted between 30 and 45 degrees from true vertical.

Ladder bars mount to the rear axle housing slightly inboard from the frame rails and mount to the chassis closer to the middle of the vehicle. This design does more to gain traction than provide a soft ride; therefore, it is used primarily for hot rods that may occasionally see some drag racing action.

If you are looking more for comfort than superior traction, you should choose radius rods or a four-link suspension. A radius rod mounts to the rear axle in two locations, while pivoting from the frame rail at one location. A parallel four-link works the same way; however, it mounts to the frame rail in two locations. Pivoting from two locations causes the rear axle housing to move in more of an up-and-down motion during suspension travel, whereas pivoting from one location produces an arc motion. Radius rods or a parallel four-link require the use of a panhard rod, while a triangulated four-link does not. The triangulated four-link uses two bars to connect the rear axle housing to the frame rail. The two upper bars mount to the rear axle housing and then mount to a location on the chassis inboard of the two lower bars.

Pete & Jake's offers its "Viper" coilovers, which are available in polished or plain aluminum finish. The correct coilover is based on the weight of your vehicle. Although coilovers are adjustable, the correct spring rate goes a long way toward obtaining the optimum ride. Ask guys with finished cars similar to yours for their recommendation on what spring rate to use. *Pete & Jake's Hot Rod Parts*

Independent Just because a hot rod is rear-wheel drive does not mean that it has to ride rough. There is no better complement to an independent front suspension than an independent rear suspension. By the very nature of their design, most independent rear suspensions are not as bulky looking as many of their forward counterparts. For this reason, they are equally fashionable on early and later cars.

Two relatively common OEM independent rear suspensions come from the Jaguar and the Corvette. When purchasing this type of rear suspension, make sure you get all of the parts, as it all installs as a unit, unlike the components for a solid rear axle. Although expensive compared to a nonindependent rear, an independent rear will smooth out the ride and look even better. Although most independent rears are chrome plated (adding to their cost), they can be detailed with paint, as long as it is complemented with some sparkle.

Some hot rod companies are now manufacturing complete independent rear suspensions. Often based on a nine-inch Ford rearend and Corvette suspension, these new suspensions will provide plenty of cushion while adequately handling all of the power you can put to them.

Heidt's Superide IRS is available with most of the parts fully polished for the ultimate in good looks. Utilizing Corvette bearing assemblies, Ford 9-inch third member, and inboard Wilwood disc brakes, this kit offers the ultimate in ride, strength, and roadability. Heidt's Hot Rod Shop

Wheelbase

As you are assembling your chassis, whether it is original, reproduction, buggy sprung, or fully independent, you need to verify that the wheelbase is correct. The wheelbase should be the same on each side of the car. You would be surprised at how many are off slightly.

Most of the error is probably accumulated in the final assembly stage. As an example, on a hot rod with a four-link front suspension, two separate bars locate one front wheel, while two more locate the other front wheel. If the two upper bars are not the same length and the two lower bars are the same length, the front axle will not be perpendicular to the vehicle's centerline. Likewise with the rear axle. Although it is easy to get the axles in crooked, there is no reason for it. You should have the axles in the car straight before you go any further. Don't expect a wheel alignment to correct faulty chassis building.

DRIVETRAIN

Automobile engines of all designs and manufacture have been put between the frame rails of a hot rod at one time or another. Finding the right one for you depends largely on your personal preferences and finances.

As the very nature of hot rodding is to increase performance, it would seem appropriate that the engine should be powerful. However, the engine is only a portion of the performance equation. Using an appropriate transmission, the correct rear end gear ratio, and appropriate tires is important too.

Increased performance is relative. Although most contemporary hot rods are running small block Chevrolet engines, a fuel-injected or blown four- or six-cylinder engine is a hot rod compared to stock. Many of these seemingly boring engines can be built to crank out some serious horsepower. Put the right gearing behind them and they will flat out surprise you.

Engine

The focal point of most any hot rod will be the engine. Whether you have a fully polished blower with a couple of 800 cfm carburetors or a single four barrel sitting atop your engine, it needs to run good and look good. In deciding what type of motor you put between the frame rails and how much power it should put out, you have many options.

Before you buy your engine or any pieces for it, you need to decide what it is that you really want the engine to do.

Perhaps you want the engine to be the primary focal spot of your hot rod. A blower with dual four barrels will get you some attention, but it will cost you some money. You have to ask yourself if you want to spend the money and if you can even think about using all of the horsepower it can create. If you have the horsepower, you need to have the suspension to put the power to the pavement. There is nothing wrong with horsepower—just realize that the quest for it is the beginning of a domino effect.

If you don't need or want tremendous horsepower but still want to gain attention, clean and detail the engine. You don't have to chrome everything under the hood to make it look good. Far from it. Well-prepped, properly assembled, painted exterior components, combined with neatly routed, correct-length plug wires and hoses go a long way in the looks department. The correct amount of painted (or powder-coated) pieces with a tasteful amount of polished (chromed, stainless, or billet) components looks great.

New crate engines are available from the big manufacturers. This 330-horsepower deluxe from General Motors Performance includes the carburetor, distributor, and plug wires.

consistent within the small block and big block classes for each manufacturer. Thus, a smallblock Chevy—whether 265, 283, 327 or 350 cubic inches—has a length of 26.5 inches, while a big block (396, 427, 454) or straight six Chevy is four inches longer. The width of that same small block Chevy is 19.5 inches, while the Chrysler Hemi is the widest at 28.5 inches. Ford, Buick, Oldsmobile, Cadillac, and Pontiac engines all fit between these extremes for length and width.

A difference in length of four inches may not sound like a lot, but remember that you need to fit a fan, a radiator, and a distributor cap ahead of the engine. When measuring for width, include room for headers and steering components to run alongside the engine.

Even though racers say that nothing beats cubic inches, most any engine block is capable of being modified to produce more horsepower than any street-able hot rod can put to the pavement anyway. For all intents and purposes, any engine producing more than 400 horsepower is overkill in a street-driven hot rod. That is not to say we would mind driving one.

Crate motor

One of the advantages of the popularity of hot rodding today is the availability of complete, brand-new engines, ready to be installed between the frame rails of your favorite hot rod. For some, the sticker price may seem hard to swallow, but being able to buy a complete engine for around three grand is less expensive than rebuilding one. Unless you find an engine that is in perfect condition in the first place, the cost of rebuilding it will usually exceed the cost of buying a new crate motor. That wasn't always the case, but it is today. From a wide variety of small block Chevrolet engines and a growing number of Ford offerings to a complete blown Chrysler Hemi, crate motors are much more common than just a few years ago.

These crate motors are available in varying degrees of completeness, so be sure that you read the fine print about what is included before you part with your money. A common package is a long block that contains the block, the heads, an oil pan, and all of the internal workings. If valve covers are included, they will usually be plain and usually (but not always) be replaced with something better looking by most hot rodders. Since there are still more items required to get this engine running, it is at the relative low end of the buy-in scale. If you want a crate motor but can't justify or budget that one big expense at once, this is the way to go.

Moving up the line, more complete and expensive crate motors will typically start to include the intake manifold, the distributor, the water pump, and sometimes a carburetor. Most crate motors do not include exhaust manifold(s), spark plug wires, pulleys, belts, or throttle linkage.

Brand Engines from most any branch of the big three automakers can be made to fit between the frame rails of a hot rod. However, as simple as it may seem, some will fit with less trouble than others will. There is no denying that small block Chevrolet engines are popular with hot rodders. They are slightly smaller in physical size than most of their counterparts; they are common, and therefore less expensive; and aftermarket parts are readily available. For someone who is more interested in getting a car on the road than being unique, a Chevrolet engine is a practical solution.

If you are building anything other than a Chevy hot rod, you may choose to be a brand loyalist when it comes to an engine. There is a certain amount of honor in that. Realize from the start, however, that you may be required to fabricate you own motor mounts, modify the inner fender panels, and recontour the firewall just to fit the engine. This is more of a problem on earlier cars than later ones.

Size Although most V-8 engines are available in a wide variety of displacements, their physical size is typically

This well-detailed engine looks great with its nicely painted block, complemented by polished valve covers, intake manifold, and air cleaner.

For something a little different, the builder of this early Chevrolet coupe installed a Mopar Hemi engine between the frame rails. Although clearance would be tight, installing a hood would not be as impossible as it may look. The hood may require a bulge to clear the alternator and possibly the forward edge of the valve covers, as well as an opening up top for the air cleaner.

Rebuilt

There is absolutely nothing wrong with rebuilding an engine yourself or having it done. Unless you have a very well-equipped shop or an endless line of credit, chances are that the rebuild will involve a little of both. Many rodders can do the disassembly, cleanup, and reassembly but will have machine work done by someone else. What you can do yourself and what you will pay for is for you to decide. Even though you may be able to do the work, you may not have the time. You decide.

You first will need to find a decent engine block. This can be from a salvage yard, a swap meet, or a classified ad or can even be a new bare block from a mail-order business such as Summit Racing or Jeg's. Depending on

A small block Chevrolet engine with three deuces and plenty of chrome complements the style of this nostalgic coupe quite nicely.

Looking for a complete engine for your hot rod? Several companies besides General Motors and Ford offer complete engines, ready for installation between your favorite set of frame rails.

where you purchase the block, you will need to do as much inspection as you can to verify that it is indeed rebuidable. A low-mileage engine out of a wrecked car in a salvage yard may be a safer bet than a swap meet special that has oblong cylinders. Don't hesitate to invite someone you trust to give a second opinion before you part with your hard-earned cash.

Soon after buying an engine block, if not before, you need to be scouting around for a machine shop to do the machining that you can't. Although it is your engine, it will be a good idea to ask if the machinist has any specific recommendations regarding parts selection. Providing them with an accurate idea of what kind of hot rod you are building and what you expect from it will help determine how much machining will

"Veteran" engines can be found in classified ads, salvage yards, and swap meets. This swap meet special is a 1958, 348-cubic-inch Chevrolet, offered for 500 bucks or best offer.

March Performance Pulleys offers a serpentine belt pulley system for those who choose to run one drive belt. This configuration runs the water pump, air conditioning compressor, and alternator from the crank. March Performance Pulleys

need to be done. Depending on what you are starting with and what you want, a cleaned up bore with slightly oversized pistons may be adequate, while a completely blueprinted engine will be necessary for others—and you can bet we're talking more than a couple of bucks difference between the two extremes. Keep in mind that an engine builder who builds nothing but drag race engines may not be the ideal choice for building your fairgrounds cruiser. Likewise, a shop that cranks out nothing but stock rebuilt engines may not be an ideal choice for your maximum-fun hot rod.

Along with an engine block, you will need to start gathering all of the necessary parts. Everything from an oil

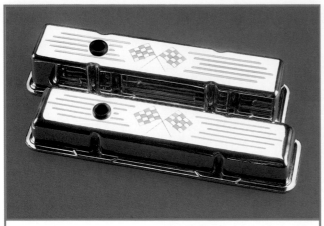

Dress-up valve covers may be a necessary purchase, whether you're installing a rebuilt motor or a basic crate engine. Billet Specialties

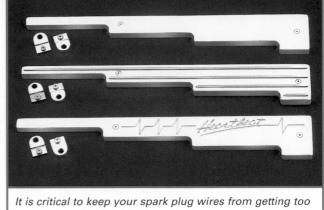

It is critical to keep your spark plug wires from getting too close to your exhaust system. These spark plug wire looms mount to the valve covers and keep the plug wires organized. Billet Specialties

This raised rib-style air cleaner is designed for use with a dual-quad carb setup. Billet Specialties

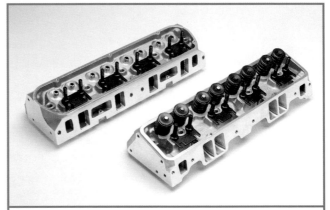

Cylinder heads are available as bare heads or as complete assemblies. Bare heads are less costly initially but require additional parts and assembly. Edelbrock

pan (don't forget the drain plug) to the carburetor and from the cooling fan to the pressure plate will be necessary. The good thing about a rebuilt engine is that you can budget your parts buying as necessary. Yes, being short on cash makes the process take longer.

Transmission

So do you want to shift gears for yourself, or do you want the transmission to do that for you? An automatic will be less complicated to install; however, a stick shift might be more your style when cruisin' around town. An automatic will require a linkage between the shifter and transmission, but that is usually more flexible in location than the clutch pedal and linkage of a stick shift.

Like the engine, the transmission can be purchased either new or rebuilt. A new transmission will be all nice and clean,

ready for paint or polish; however, it may be lacking some of the components that you really need to make it work. When ordering a new transmission, or even a rebuilt one, be sure to ask if such items as the flywheel, torque converter, clutch, and speedometer sender are included.

If you are buying an engine from a salvage yard or a swap meet, you may want to buy the transmission out of the same vehicle at the same time if it's the type you plan to run in your hot rod. This will help avoid compatibility problems later on. If it's from an old vehicle, keep in mind that both automatic and manual transmissions have come a long way over the decades in terms of feel and performance. Of course, you may be into an older-style setup, in which event you can go for whatever meets your needs. With an obscure engine, like an aluminum Buick/Olds 215 V-8, buying the tranny that comes with it assures you of something that fits without adapters.

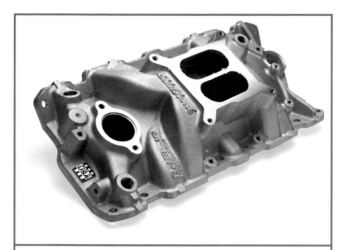

One of the pioneers of hot rodding, Edelbrock offers an extensive line of intake manifolds. Edelbrock

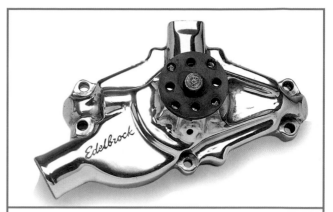

A water pump will also be necessary to keep coolant pumping through your engine. This polished unit will certainly dress up the front portion of your engine compartment. Edelbrock

For those who don't want to adjust their carburetors all the time, the Edelbrock Performer carb is a good choice. Properly adjusted right out of the box, this carb is a winner. Edelbrock

When choosing the particular components of the drivetrain (engine, transmission, and rearend gears), you must look at the big picture to achieve the combination that gives the best performance (and therefore the best economy). Everyone knows that 4.11:1 gears will be quick off the line; however, if those gears are not paired with the ideal tire size, they may not be as quick as you think.

The builder of this coupe included a kit to simulate the look of Buick drum brakes, providing a nostalgic look with the stopping power of discs.

Rear

Just because the front brakes do the majority of the braking doesn't mean you can get away without brakes on the rear axle. On most hot rods, drum brakes on the rear will be sufficient, although rear disc brakes may give you more piece of mind while you are cruisin' around town in your pride and joy.

Disc As more late-model vehicles are being equipped with rear disc brakes as standard equipment, there are more donors for hot rods. Like front disc brakes, rear disc brakes are easy to install, are becoming more common, and are easy enough to maintain. Although rear disc brakes aren't as critical to stopping as front disc brakes are, in a panic stop they may make the difference. After owning a hot rod Model A Tudor with four-wheel disc brakes, I can't imagine driving a hot rod with anything less.

Drum Most any rear axle that is used under a hot rod is available with drum brakes. Therefore, if you are buying a rear end from a salvage yard or at a swap meet, it may very well already have the drum brakes included with the deal. This is fine and will save a considerable amount of money over buying a disc brake kit. Realize that you may need to

rebuild the brakes for them to work properly; however, the necessary parts will more than likely be in stock at your local auto parts store.

Other components

Since modern-day braking systems are operated hydraulically, a few other components are necessary to make the entire brake system operate correctly. Brake fluid stored in the master cylinder has to flow to each of the brakes (whether disc or drum) whenever pressure is applied to the brake pedal.

Master cylinder There are two basic designs of master cylinders: a single reservoir and a dual reservoir. Although the most common single reservoir type (often referred to as a "fruit jar") was found on early Mustangs, it is no longer popular. With this single reservoir type, a leak in the brake system would disable the entire system. With the more popular dual reservoir type, a leak would disable only the front or rear brakes, depending on which system had the leak.

The master cylinder is where the brake fluid is stored. Therefore, its location is important for a couple of reasons. You must be able to pour brake fluid into the master cylinder with a minimum of trouble. You will need to do this before you drive your hot rod, and may need to top it off after you bleed the brakes. Using a remote-fill master cylinder may be necessary (or at least more convenient) if you are required to fill the master cylinder very often. The location of the master cylinder will also dictate whether you must install residual check valves in the system (refer to the section on residual check valves below).

Typically in hot rods, the master cylinder is mounted on the firewall or beneath the floor. If it is mounted on the firewall, it will be visible in the engine compartment. Newer hot rods usually have more available room in the engine compartment, so this is a natural location. If it is mounted under the floor (typical on earlier hot rods), it will be out of sight, yet it may be difficult to service. Oftentimes, this is a necessity. This is merely one instance of something that should be well thought out beforehand.

Pedal The brake pedal is what provides input from the driver to pressurize the brake fluid in the master cylinder to operate the brakes. If the master cylinder is mounted below the floor, the pedal must move through a slotted hole in the floor. Be sure that adequate clearance is available for the brake pedal to swing through its entire motion.

Power booster (optional) Mounted to the master cylinder, a brake booster is what provides "power brakes." Fed off vacuum, the typical source is through a vacuum line to the carburetor. Power boosters can vary in size from

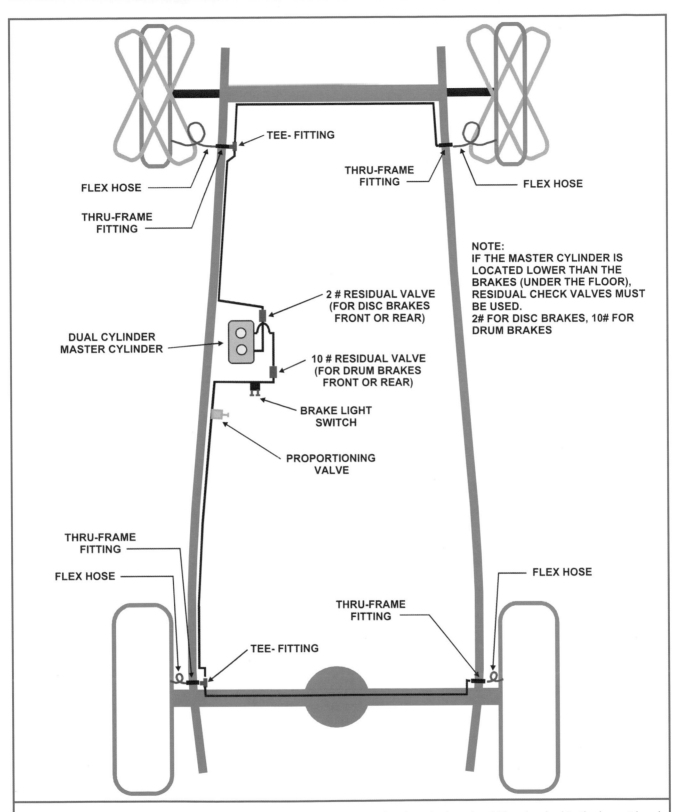

TEE- FITTING

THRU-FRAME
FITTING

FLEX HOSE

FLEX HOSE

THRU-FRAME
FITTING

NOTE:
IF THE MASTER CYLINDER IS
LOCATED LOWER THAN THE
BRAKES (UNDER THE FLOOR),
RESIDUAL CHECK VALVES MUST
BE USED.
2# FOR DISC BRAKES, 10# FOR
DRUM BRAKES

2 # RESIDUAL VALVE
(FOR DISC BRAKES
FRONT OR REAR)

DUAL CYLINDER
MASTER CYLINDER

10 # RESIDUAL VALVE
(FOR DRUM BRAKES
FRONT OR REAR)

BRAKE LIGHT
SWITCH

PROPORTIONING
VALVE

THRU-FRAME
FITTING

FLEX HOSE

FLEX HOSE

THRU-FRAME
FITTING

TEE- FITTING

This diagram gives a basic overview of typical brake line routing. Note that front brakes should be plumbed to the largest bowl of the master cylinder. An option for the rear axle brake line is to run the hard line partially across the rear crossmember, then run one flex line to a T-fitting mounted on the rear axle housing. Hard lines are then run to each rear brake.

about seven to twelve inches in diameter. With room often being a valuable commodity in a hot rod, a smaller power booster is usually better.

Some people may insist on using a brake booster, while others may not. It will be more useful in a larger fat-fendered sedan than a lighter highboy. Personal preference is probably the key; however, you should check with other guys who have hot rods similar to yours before you make a definite decision.

Proportioning valve The proportioning valve is mounted inline with the rear brake line. A knob allows you to open or close the valve infinitely to fine-tune the brakes to obtain the correct front-to-rear bias.

With hot rods having most of their weight on the front axle, big and little tire combinations, and disproportionate power-to-weight ratios, a proportioning valve can be a necessity. Use the valve to fine-tune your brakes after driving your hot rod. Be careful not to send too much stopping power to the rear brakes—under heavy braking this can cause the rear brakes to lock and send your hot rod into a spin.

Residual check valve A residual check valve keeps a slight pressure on the brake line at all times to keep the brake fluid from running away from the discs or drums and back into the master cylinder. If the master cylinder is located higher than the brake cylinders (on the firewall), the residual check valves aren't necessary, as gravity does the job automatically. If the master cylinder is mounted lower than the brake cylinders (beneath the floor), these check valves are necessary.

Residual check valves are mounted inline with the brake lines and are usually located within approximately 12 inches of the master cylinder. Check valves are available in two-pound or ten-pound ratings. Whether they are going to the front or the rear brakes, disc brakes require a two-pound (2#) valve, while drum brakes require a ten-pound (10#) valve.

Hoses Brake line hoses can be rubber or braided stainless steel. As long as they are the correct length to work, while allowing the front wheels to turn, and don't leak, either type will work just fine. Braided stainless may look better, but it's more expensive. Rubber hoses may not look as "high tech," but they are less expensive and will be easier to replace when you need one in Waytoheckandgone, Utah.

Brake lines Like hoses, brake lines are available plain or fancy. Standard OEM brake line tubing is available at any auto parts store worthy of being called a parts store and therefore is relatively inexpensive. It is easy to flare, easy to bend and, when scuffed with some steel wool and sprayed

This photo shows a dual master cylinder and a power booster. Vacuum from a source such as the carburetor will be necessary for the booster to work properly. Heidt's Hot Rod Shop

with some clear paint, looks good too. Stainless tubing looks great; however, it's pretty much the opposite of the OEM brake line. Once you get the knack of working with it, it's not bad, but the beginner should probably avoid trying to flare or bend stainless tubing.

Brake line clamps Whether you choose billet aluminum, nylon, or rubber coated, you'll need clamps of some sort to secure the brake line. Brake lines that are not securely attached to the chassis will eventually work loose, causing leaks. Brake lines should also not be allowed to rub on the chassis or any other components, as the chafing may ultimately cause a leak that is difficult to find.

Brake light switch

Two different types of brake light switches are typical on hot rods. Both have two electrical contacts to which wires to the brake lights are connected. One kind of brake light switch closes when the brake pedal is pushed against it. This type will require some adjustment to position it properly so that the brake lights will come on the instant the brake pedal is depressed. The other type of brake light switch is mounted inline and operates based on the brake fluid passing through it. This latter type should be avoided if using silicone brake fluid, as the silicone wreaks havoc on the electrical contacts, without giving any sort of warning of failure.

WHEEL/TIRE COMBINATION

Other than the finished paint, nothing else makes as big a visual impact on a hot rod as the wheel and tire combination. Even while a hot rod is in primer, the just-right stance provided by big and little tires, and the way the wheels and tires fit into a fender, can make a big difference.

When using a disc/drum brake combination, it is recommended that you use a proportioning valve to dial in the correct amount of brake force to each axle. Residual check valves are located in the brake line near the master cylinder. Heidt's Hot Rod Shop

As the name implies, thru-frame fittings allow the brake line to pass through the frame. Hard brake line is run into the inside, while a flexible hose runs from the outside to the backing plate or the caliper. Billet Specialties

To prevent chafing, brake and fuel lines must be securely attached to the chassis of your hot rod. Available in a variety of styles and prices, these aluminum clamps thread directly into the frame rail, securing the line between the two pieces. Billet Specialties

Some builders prefer to use an inline brake light switch that is activated by internal line pressure. Two downsides are that they can be a possible source for a fluid leak (any connection in the brake line is a suspect), and they do not last very long with systems utilizing silicon brake fluid. Sadly, they give no indication of failure.

With the wide variety of sizes and styles, it is necessary to think of the wheels and tires as a combination rather than independently. Back when most wheels were 14 or 15 inches in diameter, most any tire would look good on most any wheel. Not a big deal. However, all that has changed. With the availability of wheels in the 20- to 24-inch range, the entire concept of a hot rod can be changed. Once upon a time, switching between a set of steelies with wide whites and a set of Halibrands with dirt track tires was the big deal to change a rod's appearance for the weekend. Today, we can switch between a set of 15-inch steelies and 20-plus-inch billet wheels to change a rod's appearance drastically.

Wheels

With wheels ranging in price from about fifty bucks for an unpainted steelie to close to a grand for a custom, polished billet piece, what you run becomes important. Although you can hardly build any hot rod for the price of another guy's wheels and tires anymore, that price difference can sometimes determine whether you finish your hot rod or not. You should also realize that you don't

61

What goes around comes around. Wheels make the difference in a car's look, but what is popular one day may not be the next. Polished wheels look good on many a car, but painted steelies in a contrasting color look just as good on this primered coupe.

A more traditional design, yet still billet, is this "Legacy" wheel, also from Billet Specialties. Billet Specialties

have to have those high-dollar wheels on your hot rod unless you want to. Having an idea of how you want the finished vehicle to look before you do any building will help you determine which wheels to buy.

A practical thing to do is to buy a set of steelies with the correct size and offset to use during construction. If you scratch or dent a low-dollar steelie, it's not a big deal; however, if you damage a high-dollar custom wheel, it will hurt.

Tires

An important factor in choosing the right tire and wheel combination is how well the tire fills the fender. The fenders need to be filled to look right. All too often, there is too much room between the tire and the fender. Difficult to imagine perhaps, but quite obvious when you see an example of it. Of course, you need to have adequate clearance between tire and fender.

As you are strolling through your next rod run, make notes of what size tires and wheels are on rods that you like. Soon you will start to notice a trend as to what looks right and what doesn't on any particular body style.

With this coupe being somewhat racer inspired (side pipes and injector-style scoop), race wheels such as ET-IIIs are an appropriate choice.

Whether you are running steel or billet wheels, the wheel and tire need to fill the fender. You must maintain adequate clearance, yet to have the "look," the fenders need to be filled.

OUT IN THE GARAGE
Installing an aftermarket Mustang II–type front suspension

One of the most common methods of installing an independent front suspension in a hot rod is to use a Mustang II front crossmember and control arms. These particular cars were manufactured from 1974 through 1978. Original crossmembers may be getting scarce now; however, several different companies are reproducing them for the hot rod industry. The rest of the suspension components are being reproduced as well, even though many of them are still readily available over the counter at your local auto parts store.

One of the companies that manufactures new front suspension kits based on the Mustang II is Heidt's Hot Rod Shop. Its kit is available in a variety of price levels, from plain steel control arms to be painted, all the way up to fully polished stainless steel control arms. No matter which kit you choose, the installation is essentially the same. For the lowdown on how to install one of Heidt's kits, we follow along as Keith Moritz at Morfab Customs installs one in a 1941 Chevrolet pickup frame.

1

Prior to our arrival at Morfab Customs, Keith had already welded in the front crossmember and spring hats. It is highly recommended to have the frame sitting level on jack stands before installing the front suspension. Different vehicles and different suspension manufacturers will have different methods of locating the crossmember, so refer to the instructions before welding anything in place. Remember, measure twice, cut (or weld) once. If you are retrofitting an original frame, the front crossmember should be in the same location as the original front axle, so you may transfer that location prior to removing the original front suspension.

2

This photo shows the boxing plate and the spring hat for the passenger side of the vehicle. The boxing plates (included with Heidt's kit) are actually welded in place between the upper and lower flanges of the frame rail before the cross member is welded in. Another point worth mentioning is the "C" cut in the frame rails to allow for the rack and pinion steering. The "C" is cut out of the frame rail and the boxing plate and then boxed in by welding in a semicircular piece of round tubing, supplied with the kit. The spring hat is also located per the instructions for your particular application.

3

With the boxing plates, crossmember, and spring hats welded in place, assembly of the bolt-on components may begin. (Note: In this particular instance, final welding was already completed. If you are installing an independent front suspension for the first time, it would be wise to first tack-weld the crossmember and related components in place. Then install the rest of the suspension and the front sheet metal to verify that the wheels are centered in the wheelwells and that the wheelbase is correct. Don't forget to go back and finish the welding!) *Each of the lower control arms is secured to the crossmember with a long bolt, washers, and a lock nut. The rod shown protruding from the control arm (horizontal in the photo) is a simulated shock. More about this just a little bit later. Due to the length of the bolt securing the control arm, it may need a little bit of persuasion to go in all the way.*

4

The upper control arm is now secured in place with T-bolts through the spring hat, through the control arm, and secured with a lock nut. Slots in the spring hat allow for the position of the control arm to be adjusted to provide proper wheel alignment. These slots will provide the caster and camber adjustments. Be sure to ask for the proper alignment specs for your hot rod when you purchase your independent front suspension.

5

Keith now installs the passenger side upper control arm in the same manner as on the driver's side. Again, the long bolt may need a bit of hammer persuasion to go all the way through the control arm. Go ahead and tighten the nut completely.

6

The upper control arm is installed the same way as on the driver's side. Typically, the upper control arms are outward more on the front than the back; however, before the vehicle is driven very much, it should be aligned with proper alignment equipment.

7

Remember that simulated shock? It is much too early in the buildup of this particular hot rod to install the shocks or especially the coil springs. Most rodders will use a piece of threaded rod in place of a shock during this mock-up time. A threaded rod can inadvertently be loosened or tightened, however, thereby having at least a minor effect on the accuracy of your mock-up. Keith uses a piece of steel tubing cut to a predetermined length, with a length of threaded rod welded to the upper end of it. This will keep the lower control arm parallel with the ground (as it should be) and simulate the actual ride height.

8

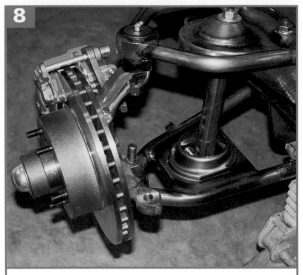

Prior to actually tightening the nut onto the top of the "shock," the spindle should be secured to the lower and then the upper ball joints.

9

Be sure to tighten the nuts on the ball joints sufficiently to install a cotter pin. When driving, these ball joints are subject to severe vibration, so it is mandatory to install cotter pins in case the nut vibrates loose. The rotor and brake calipers may be installed at this time too, if you like. Whether you do it now or later, be sure to pack the wheel bearings (inner and outer) with grease before driving the vehicle. Also, be sure to install a cotter pin in the spindle to make sure that the rotor does not separate itself from the spindle.

10

With both spindles installed and secured, the rack and pinion steering may be installed. Whether power or manual, the rack typically mounts to the crossmember with two bolts. Verify that the steering input shaft (with yellow protective cover in this photo) is pointed toward the passenger compartment, and then tighten the bolts completely.

11

Once you've made sure you haven't mounted the rack completely backward (that would be fairly obvious), its installation consists of tightening two bolts.

12

Keith now attaches the tie rod ends to the spindles. Be sure to install cotter pins on this connection as well. Having a tie rod end come loose while driving down the interstate is no fun . . . trust me.

13

When attaching the tie rod ends to the spindle, it may be necessary to lengthen or shorten the tie rods. Don't worry, you do not need to cut or weld anything on to them. Simply loosen the jamb nut securing the tie rod end, and thread it in (to shorten the tie rod) or out (to lengthen the tie rod).

14

Just be sure that each tie rod is within one turn of being the same length on each side. Again, don't forget the cotter pins.

CHASSIS

Now is a good time to double-check that the upper control arms are tight in the spring hats. They will need to be adjusted when the vehicle is aligned, but the alignment shop will be able to do that. Anytime the vehicle is moving, the control arms need to be tight to the spring hat or the crossmember.

With the tie rods connecting both spindles, the chassis can easily become a rolling chassis with the addition of a set of wheels and tires. Even if you don't use the wheels and tires that you plan on using on your finished hot rod, being able to easily move the chassis around in the shop will be a plus.

At this point, it is not essential that the toe is set correctly; however, it should be fairly close. With tie rods connected to both spindles, the rotors should be roughly parallel when pointed forward.

CHASSIS

Installing a leaf spring rear suspension

Although coilover suspensions are very popular for the rear end of a hot rod, some rodders prefer to use a parallel leaf spring arrangement. The parallel springs are more commonly found on later model hot rods and on pickup trucks. A benefit of using parallel leaf springs is that lowering blocks can easily be installed to lower the back end of your hot rod to just where you want it.

To see how easily a set of parallel leaf springs is installed, we follow along as Keith Moritz of Morfab Customs installs a set in the same 1941 Chevrolet pickup that received the Mustang II front suspension. One of the great things about early hot rods (whether car or truck) is that the frames are very similar (if not indeed identical), so a modification that works on one vehicle will be very typical of so many others.

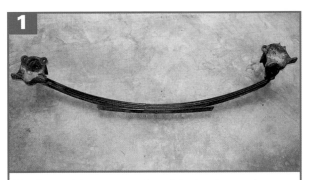

1 The first task is to remove the original springs and rear axle from the vehicle. Typically, the original spring hangers are riveted to the outside and the bottom of the frame rail. The heads of the rivets can usually be ground off and then the rivet driven out with a hammer and punch. Use caution not to grind excessive amounts of the frame rail from around the rivet. More than likely, you are not going to reuse the original springs, so don't even bother taking them out of the spring hangers.

2 To get the rear wheels centered in the wheelwell, it helps to have the rear fender bolted into position and the frame sitting level. Trying to do this accurately without the fender will cause you more work than necessary. Keith first measures the lowest portion of the wheel opening. From what would be the center of the measurement, a plumb bob is hung from the fender and secured with a piece of masking tape. The measurement is double-checked with the plumb bob.

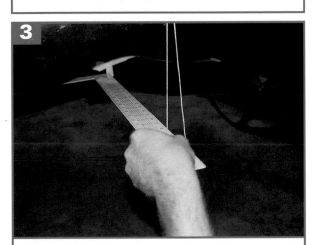

3 With the plumb bob hanging from the center of the wheel opening of the fender, a carpenter's square is used to mark the axle centerline on the frame rail and a vertical line scribed. Measurements for the new spring hangers can now be located from this line.

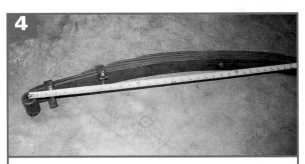

4 On the new springs, the front hanger eyelet will be curled upward when on the vehicle, while the rear eyelet will be curled in the opposite direction. The new springs will also have a centering pin that will locate the springs with the spring pad that will later be welded to the axle housing. From the centering pin, measure to the center of the front eyelet to determine how far the front spring hanger must be from the axle centerline.

69

5

From the vertical line scribed on the frame rails (this should be done on each frame rail), measure forward along the frame rail the same distance as the measurement of the front portion of the spring. Transfer this measurement to the lower flange of the frame rail and weld on the new spring hanger. It is recommended that you simply tack-weld the brackets in at this point and finish-weld only after you've checked the completed installation to make sure the wheels are placed accurately in the wheelwell, the axle is square in the frame, and the springs are not in a bind.

6

The new springs should have the correct amount of arch built into them, so measure from the front eye of the spring to the rear eye. Measure from the front spring bracket rearward along the frame rail this same distance to establish the location for the rear spring hanger. Tack-weld this bracket in place. Be sure to mount the hanger so it is square with the axle and frame.

7

The front eye of the spring can now be secured directly to the front spring hanger with a bolt and lock nut. Be sure to install all of the spring hanger bolts in the same direction.

8

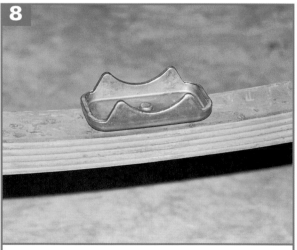

The spring pads can now be mounted onto the springs. The centering pin in the springs simply fits into the corresponding hole in the pads. Before securing the spring to the rear spring hanger, the rear axle housing should be positioned between the frame rails and the springs, resting in the spring pad. Originally, the axle was usually located beneath the spring; however, most hot rodders lower the back of the car the diameter of the axle housing simply by putting the spring below the axle.

9

The rear of the spring is secured to the spring hanger with a spring shackle. This shackle allows a slight amount of movement by the rear axle to avoid damaging the frame or drivetrain.

10

With the rear axle housing being lifted by a floor jack, the rear of the springs can now be secured to the rear spring hanger with the spring shackle. Install the shackle plate and secure with a lock nut on each stud.

11

Before installing the U-bolts and lower shock mount, verify that the axle housing is properly located from side to side, and that the pinion angle is close. Keith suggests not actually welding the spring pads to the rear axle housing until the engine is in the vehicle, the intended wheels and tires are bolted on, and the vehicle is at proper ride height. This will ensure that the pinion angle is correct.

12

The lower shock mount should be installed with the stud for the shock to the rear of the vehicle. By placing shims between the spring pad and the top of the springs, the vehicle can be lowered by the thickness of the shims.

13

The mount is then secured with four lock nuts.

14

From the opposite side, we can get a better look at the lower shock mount.

15

Keith will still have to construct or modify an upper crossmember to be a suitable upper shock mount. The crossmember should span between both frame rails and have upper shock mounts located so that the shock is mounted at approximately 30 degrees from true vertical.

72

Installing a four-link and coilover rear suspension

On early hot rods, a four-link and coilover rear suspension is very common. It is easy to install, works well, and generally looks good under a slender-fendered or highboy hot rod. It will have all of those benefits under a fat-fendered hot rod, but it is not as common for that application.

A typical four-link kit consists of the four bars and rod ends, frame brackets for the front end of the bars, and brackets to mount the bars to the rear axle housing. Also necessary, but not always included in the kit, are the coilovers, the upper crossmember and/or coilover mounts, and a panhard rod. *(Note: A panhard rod is not needed if the four-link is triangulated.)*

Keith Moritz at Morfab Customs was installing a triangulated four-link and coilovers in the back of one of his own reproduction 1934 Ford frames. Follow along as we see how this is done.

Keith already has the frame sitting level on jack stands. It was known from the start that this frame would receive this particular rear suspension, so while the frame was still in the chassis jig, a rear crossmember designed specifically for coilovers was installed and welded in place. The Morfab Customs crossmember features two sets of mounting holes for adjusting the angle of the coilovers. Keith locates the rear axle housing by measuring from the front crossmember. With the center of the front crossmember being the front axle centerline, this will establish the correct wheelbase.

One end of each of the four bars will have an adjustable end. Typically, the adjustable end is mounted at the frame rather than at the axle. Bars are often shipped with the adjusters threaded almost all the way into the bar. Most adjusters have about 3 inches of thread, but to be on the safe side, completely remove one of the adjusters to see how long it really is. Then thread it back in about half way. The end shown in the photo would have plenty of adjustment if necessary to make it longer; however, it would have very little adjustment if necessary to make it shorter.

3

To assure that everything is set up precisely, suspend the rear axle housing from the frame at ride height and temporarily tack-weld it in place, using some bar stock or scrap angle. The brackets that mount the rear end of the four bars in front of the axle and the coilovers behind the axle are welded to the rear axle housing. These brackets should be positioned so that there is no binding of the four-link or the coilovers. If the four-link is mounted incorrectly, it will quickly wear out the bushings. If the coilovers bind, they are prone to breaking.

4

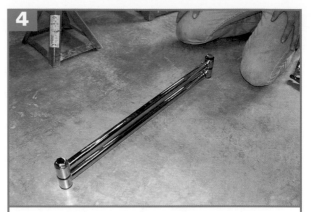

The upper bars must be adjusted to the same length and the lower bars must be adjusted to the same length, although the uppers are not necessarily the same length as the lowers. Although I don't recall ever having read or been told this before, a simple way to verify that the bars are the same is to bolt them together. If one bolt fits into the end of each bar, while another one fits through the opposite end of each bar, they are the same length. You may laugh, but you would be surprised at how many bars differ in length.

5

The nonadjustable end of the lower bar is positioned in the rear axle bracket and secured with a bolt and lock nut. Keith suggests installing the bolt so that the lock nut is to the inside for two reasons: It just plain looks nicer this way, and keeping the exposed threads of the bolt away from the tires will help prevent them from becoming gnarled up due to rocks and other debris.

6

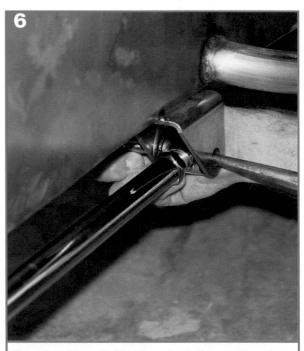

The adjustable end of the lower bar is then positioned into the frame bracket. It may take some assistance with an alignment tool to get the adjuster and the bracket aligned. When they are aligned, install the bolt and lock nut in the same direction as on the rear.

7

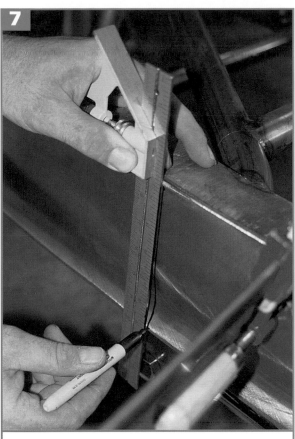

To locate the frame bracket for the upper bar, Keith projects a line up the side of the frame rail, from the center of the hole in the frame bracket. (Note: If this were a parallel four-link, the upper bars would simply mount to the upper holes of the same bracket in which the lower bars are mounted.)

8

The line is then transferred across the top and down the inside of the frame rail. This line will align with the front edge of the frame bracket for the upper (triangulated) bar.

9

With the upper bar already bolted into it, the frame bracket is clamped into place. It is now a good idea to check to see if the upper bar reaches to the intended location on the rear axle housing.

10

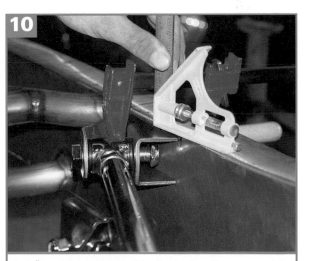

Before welding, Keith double-checks the alignment and the depth below the upper flange of the frame rail.

75

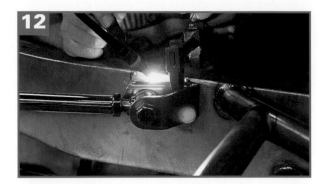

11 With all of the measurements and alignment checked, Keith tack-welds the frame bracket into place.

12 After the bracket is tacked into place, all measurements are double-checked prior to final welding.

13 After the upper rear axle housing brackets are shaped to conform more accurately to their mounting surface, they are welded in place. Note that Keith is now wearing welding gloves, as he should have been all along.

Correctly measuring for the driveshaft

Correctly measuring for a drive shaft is not difficult; however, doing it properly is critical. A couple of important things to remember are that the transmission and rear end third member that you measure between are the ones you really plan to use, and that the full weight of the vehicle should be on the suspension.

1 To connect the drive shaft to the transmission, you will need a slip yoke. Most decent auto parts stores can sell you a slip yoke, although some may have to order one for you. Tell them what kind of transmission you have (TH350, C4, Torqueflite, etc.) and they should be able to come up with the correct one. *If you will be buying the slip yoke from the company that makes the driveshaft, you can measure from the flat surface at the end of the transmission's tail shaft to the center of the pinion yoke.*

2 If you already have a slip yoke, it should be pushed onto the splines of the transmission output shaft until it bottoms out, then pulled back out ¾ inch.

3 With the slip yoke pulled out the ¾ inch from its fully seated position, measure from the center of the yoke (where the U-joint would be located) to the center of the yoke on the pinion housing.

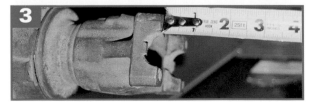

Installing front disc brakes

Whether you are using a dropped axle or independent front suspension, you should use disc brakes for stopping power on the front axle. For a quick demonstration of how to install front disc brakes, we went to Morfab Customs. Keith Moritz was installing disc brakes on a 1941 Chevy that had already been fitted with a Heidt's Mustang II front suspension.

The caliper bracket is bolted to the spindle in two places. One bolt is in the front-to-back (longitudinal) direction, while the other is in a side-to-side (lateral) direction. Be sure to use red Loctite on these bolts.

After packing the inner wheel bearing with high-temperature wheel-bearing grease, install it and the seal in the back side of the rotor. The outer bearing is then packed.

Install the outer bearing into the rotor, then slide the rotor onto the spindle.

Make sure the rotor is fully seated, and install the spindle washer on the spindle.

CHASSIS

5

Start threading the castellated nut onto the spindle, making sure that it is not cross-threaded.

6

Tighten the nut completely to seat the outer bearing, then loosen the castellated nut between a quarter and a half turn. You may need to loosen the nut slightly to align the castellated nut with the hole (in the spindle) for the cotter pin.

7

Be sure to install a cotter pin through the castellated nut and the spindle. If this cotter pin is not installed, there is nothing to keep the nut from backing off and allowing the hub/wheel assembly to part company with the vehicle.

8

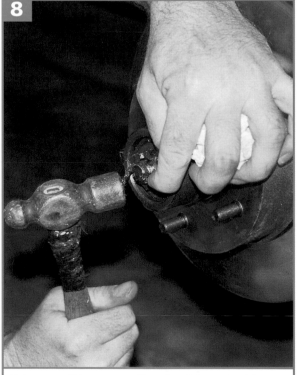

Using a small hammer or pliers, bend the ends of the cotter pin so that it doesn't slide out of position.

9

Install the dust cap and seat it with a few taps around the edge with a small hammer. Note that not having a dust cap will allow wheel-bearing grease to splatter all over your wheels.

10

Calipers vary from one manufacturer to another, but the basics are that inner and outer disc brake pads fit into the caliper.

11

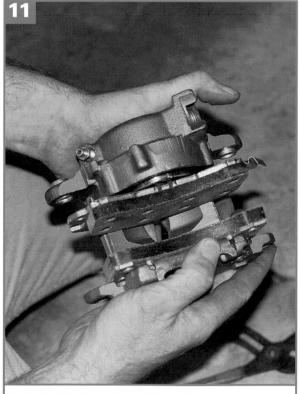

Verify that the disc pads are fully seated . . .

12

. . . and then position the caliper over the rotor.

13

Align the caliper with the mounting holes in the caliper mounting bracket and install the two slide pins.

14

The slide pins are secured in place by threads in the caliper mounting bracket.

15

Using an Allen wrench, tighten the slide pin until fully seated into the caliper mounting bracket.

16

With the rotors and calipers installed, all that is left is to plumb the brakes.

17

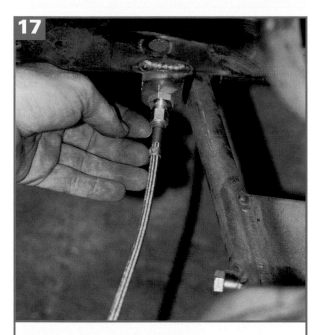

Hard brake line has been run to the frame rails. The transition to flex lines is done by a through-frame fitting, or by a bulkhead fitting through a tab under the frame as shown here. Tighten the hose securely.

18

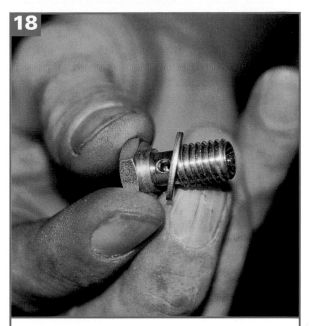

The end of the hose that connects to the caliper uses a "banjo" fitting. Brake fluid passes through the hose, into the hole in the bolt, and then through the bolt into the caliper.

A washer must be used on each side of the "banjo" fitting. Note that this bolt is actually too short for this application. It will be replaced with the correct-size bolt with the next shipment from the big brown delivery truck.

19

Thread the correct-length bolt into the caliper and tighten. Verify that the brake line hose is long enough to reach through all turning movements of the front wheels.

20

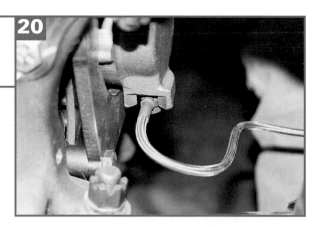

BODY ON FRAME

Now that you have the chassis at least roughed in, you should mount the body on the frame. Depending on the condition of the body at this time, it may need to be braced at the door openings and across the roof (remember that some older cars don't have a complete roof) prior to being lifted onto the chassis. Open cars will be more susceptible to flexing, simply because they lack the structural design of a coupe or sedan. On a steel-bodied vehicle, some pieces of electrical conduit (flattened on the ends) can be tack-welded across the door openings and across the inside of the body to minimize body flex. This can also be done on a fiberglass vehicle if it uses steel reinforcing. If wooden reinforcing is used, you may need to use some drywall nails to secure some wooden slats across the openings. Realize that when the body is installed for the final time (after bodywork and paint), it will not be possible to weld any bracing. On a lighter roadster body, leaving the doors in place and *latched* may be sufficient to avoid flex during the relatively short time needed to lift the body. On a coupe or sedan, you should remove the doors simply to avoid lifting the additional weight. Don't worry about painting the chassis yet, as you have plenty of time to do that later. You shouldn't have anything with final paint on it yet. Sorry, but for the best results, that is the case.

PRELIMINARY FIT

Now is the time to check the fit of all the body components. Are the wheels centered in the wheel wells? If not, what needs to be changed? Is the wheelbase of the chassis correct? If not, go back to chapter 2.

Somewhere along the line during your preliminary mockup, make a note of how far past a reference point (such as the rear axle) the body protrudes rearward. Mark that down, along with a reminder to use that figure when you get your exhaust system made up. You'll want to have your exhaust system fabricated in chapter 5, after you've assembled the chassis but before you put the body on for the final time. This figure will allow the exhaust installer to leave the tailpipe at the correct length, without your having to drive back to the muffler shop for alterations later on.

Fenders, splash aprons, and running boards

Mount the fenders, splash aprons, and running boards on the body to see how everything lines up. Note that the assembly order is different on some vehicles; for example, the front fenders and running board splash aprons go on before the body of a Ford Model A. Make notes as to how everything bolts together. You will need this information later. Look for mounting brackets or flanges that may need modification, repair, or replacement.

Keith at Morfab Customs is checking the proper location for motor mounts in this photo. This would also be the best way to install the transmission (note that transmission is missing in this photo). Bolting the engine and tranny together, then lowering them into place, has to be more convenient than lifting the tranny into place from beneath.

Lights

You can mock-up your hot rod without lights, but you can't license it that way. So if you haven't incorporated them into your design concept yet, think about them now while you're working with the body. Headlights for hot rods vary from large lights perched on a headlight bar to smaller ones mounted atop the front fenders, to others that are part of the fender/grille assembly. Brake lights can also sit in various locations and be incorporated to varying degrees into the bodywork.

This hot rod utilizes a column-mounted shifter, leaving an uninterrupted floor. Other than the gas and brake pedals, the floor space is open. A small console over the transmission tunnel houses a stereo, keeping it within easy reach of the driver or passenger.

Look at finished hot rods in the metal and in magazines, and also check out the parts catalogs. If you've sketched out your design, or are doing mock-ups with computer photo editing, add lights of different types and in various locations until you get the look you want. You don't actually need them in hand yet, but you will probably need to know where they go and how you'll secure them before you can finalize the bodywork and paint prep.

Engine

As you've no doubt discovered, moving an engine around requires an engine hoist—which you can obtain from any good auto parts store or tool rental place. To give the hoist something to grab, secure a sturdy chain to the engine with bolts of proper size and thread gauge, using appropriate heavy-gauge washers, if necessary, to stop the chain from pulling over the bolt heads. Ask the shop for details. This setup will allow you to raise and lower the engine in small

increments. Even though this arrangement should be plenty strong, don't position yourself or allow anyone else under the hanging engine. If it starts to fall, get out of the way! Everything on it is replaceable, but you and your assistants are not.

Check to see that the engine will fit in the engine compartment. Is there enough room between the engine and the firewall? Is the distributor going to be rubbing on the firewall? Will you be able to replace the distributor without pulling the body or engine? More than one firewall has been modified by a hammer. If one good blow with a hammer will provide enough room, you are probably okay, but if it requires more to gain adequate room, you need to rethink some things. If you just need to gain more room near where the distributor and firewall meet, you can cut out part of the firewall and fiberglass or weld in an inverted bulge.

If the motor mounts and transmission mounts have not yet been installed, their location should be determined now. With the engine and transmission that you plan to use (or a mock-up unit with the exact same mounting points) bolted together and supported by an engine hoist, position them between the frame rails as a unit. The location of mounts can then accurately be determined and the mounts welded in place. Although these mounts can usually be

In addition to covering the shifter, this floor console houses some A/C vents and toggle switches for the accesories. It also provides some covered storage.

moved if absolutely necessary, it is helpful to determine the best overall location for the engine and transmission, thereby setting their mounting locations. Then make everything else fit around the engine and transmission, instead of moving the engine.

As you determine engine/transmission placement, look for every other space or interference issue you can find. Is your oil pan going to hit a crossmember? Will you have access to the drain plug? Is there room for your oil filter? If you need a remote filter, look for where you'll put it. Do you have to reinforce the metal there for stability? What about steering—will the stock column get by your wide V-8 to the steering box? Probably not, in which case you'll need to reroute it with U-joints. You'll also need to get the exhaust out and down. Will that require custom headers?

Hot rodders deal with these questions all the time, and there are answers for all of them. It's important to answer them early, though, so you can make some decisions about where things need to go and what further work you'll need to do, or have done, to get them there.

Transmission

Does the floorboard of the body fit down over the transmission correctly? Most transmission-related clearance problems have to do with the chassis, but there can be problems with the body as well. Will you need to fabricate a transmission hump/driveshaft tunnel? Now is the time to decide. Realize that if you will be installing a floor shifter (standard or automatic), it will be easier to do that before the body is on the frame. This will require that a hole be cut in the floor. This hole should be large enough to access

and adjust the linkage from inside the car when finished. An access cover can then be built that attaches to the floor with small self-tapping bolts. This access cover will have a smaller hole in it for the shifter lever.

Shifter linkage

Column shift or floor shift—which do you prefer? A column shifter takes up no floor space; however, it may cause you headaches when the linkage tries to interfere with the brake pedal. A floor-mounted shifter is easy to install, especially on an automatic. It may require a console and will take up some floor space, but that may not matter. If your hot rod is going to have room for only two people in the front seat anyway, the middle of the floorboard is already vacant.

A floor-mounted shifter requires room to move, but not a gaping hole. Sheet metal filler plates along with a shifter boot can be used to keep from seeing daylight and feeling the elements through the floor.

A steering column–mounted shifter presents some unique opportunities to increase your rod building knowledge. First, the steering column shifter needs to have the same number of gears as the transmission being used. For instance, a column from an early '60s Chevrolet that was equipped with a two-speed Powerglide transmission will not work well with a late model four-speed automatic overdrive transmission. Of course, a column shifter from a car originally equipped with a manual transmission will not work well with an automatic, or vice versa. It may be possible to adapt one type of shifter to a different transmission; however, that would be beyond the scope of this book.

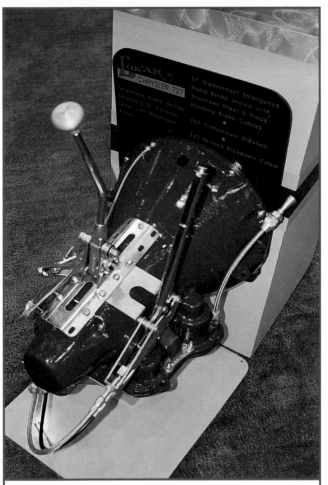

For ease of installation, a floor shifter that mounts directly to the transmission works wonders. The emergency brake lever that mounts to the transmission as well is available separately.

Notice how the grille shell is very similar to the radiator in size and shape, with very little room for movement forward or backward. Early in the process, make sure there is enough room between the radiator and the firewall for your intended engine.

An electric fan can be a room saver in a hot rod. Typically, this would be used in place of an engine-driven fan. On some vehicles, it may be necessary (or desirable) to mount a "pusher" fan in front of the radiator instead of behind it.

Available in steel or polyethylene, replacement fuel tanks, such as this tank for a 1932 Ford, may be better than trying to get all of the dirt and debris out of a gas tank that has been sitting around for years. Tanks, Inc.

Even if you are not building a 1938 Chevrolet, this polyethylene tank may work well in your nonmainstream project. Of course, it will fit in your 1938 Chevy. Don't be afraid to use a little ingenuity to make your rod building experience easier. Tanks, Inc.

To make sure that all of your interior components fit correctly, you need to install the seat(s) you intend to use. They don't need to be upholstered yet, but the framework will give a more accurate depiction than an upside-down milk crate. The author is seen here trying his former 1929 Ford Model A Tudor on for size.

Secondly, a column shifter requires some type of mechanical linkage between the steering column and the transmission. Several companies make linkages for connecting the two. However, the real-world scenario often puts the brake pedal movement into a crash course with the shifter linkage. Being able to apply the brakes only when you are in park or neutral is not an option.

Grille shell/radiator

On early hot rods, the radiator dictates the placement of the grille shell; however, that is not so much the case on later models. The two must work together, though, to supply cool air to the engine. Is there room between the engine and the radiator for a cooling fan? You will need to have some sort of a fan, whether it is driven by the engine or an electric motor. No matter how cool your hot rod is, if it overheats, it's not cool.

Hood

You will need to verify that the hood clears the engine and all of its components. Besides a blower or velocity stacks, you may need to verify that the hood will clear exhaust

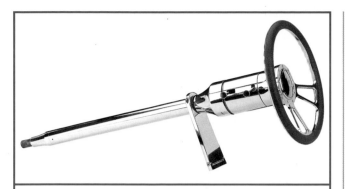

Available in polished aluminum, this steering column from Billet Specialties will highlight the interior of any hot rod. When purchasing a steering column, you will need to know what length you need and what size column drop. You will also need a steering wheel. Billet Specialties

This version of the steering column floor mount attaches from beneath the floor, giving a cleaner appearance to the interior. Billet Specialties

headers, the radiator, and various other items depending on the particular vehicle.

DETERMINING LOCATIONS

With the body on the frame, you will need to check the placement on as many different components as possible. See what will need to be moved to a different location to fit properly. You will also need to figure out the best way to mount components and how to route wiring, ducting, and plumbing. Taking this preliminary mock-up seriously will yield the best results. It is much easier and less costly to make changes at this point than it will be later.

Fuel tank(s)

It won't go if you don't have any go-juice, so a fuel tank is a necessity. Depending on the make and model of your hot rod, this may be predetermined. If it is not, or if you are really feeling creative, find a safe yet accessible place to mount the fuel tank. Keep in mind that it will need to be vented, should not be too close to excessive heat, and will need filler access.

Seats

With the body, fenders, and hood all fitting into place, it is now time to determine where all of the interior components fit best. Start by installing the seat you intend to use in its proper position. If you don't have the actual seat yet, it's better to wait until you do before fitting key controls. Sure, you could fudge it if you absolutely had to—like if you needed the car for a movie or something—but without the actual seat you won't be able to gauge perfectly how everything will feel upon completion. Choose a seat that gives you good vision and comfort and that looks appropriate for your design. Then mount it so that you have adjustment room in both directions from your ideal seating

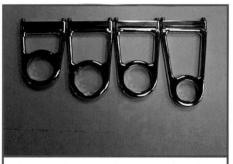

Mounting the upper end of the steering column is done with a column drop. Measure from the mounting location to the center of the steering column to determine the correct amount of drop. Mullins Steering Gears

position. Once that's in place where you can sit and see comfortably, you'll know where you want the steering wheel and pedals to go for maximum comfort.

Steering column

The steering column and steering wheel need to be located so that they are comfortable for the driver while driving. This seems obvious; however, some hot rods just are not comfortable due to a poorly placed steering column.

Securely mounting the steering column will necessitate a lower mount and an upper mount. Ideally, these two mounts would be at opposite ends of the column and as far apart as possible. The lower mount will be where the column exits the passenger compartment through the floor or firewall. The upper mount will end up extending from beneath the dash. It may be bolted directly to the dash or

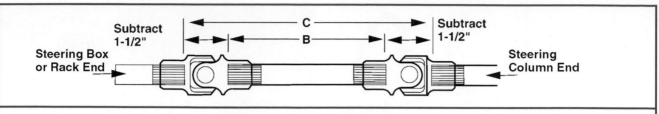

Subtract 1-1/2"

Steering Box or Rack End

C

B

Subtract 1-1/2"

Steering Column End

This diagram shows how to measure for steering shafts. Shafts that are too long or too short will cause problems.
Borgeson Universal

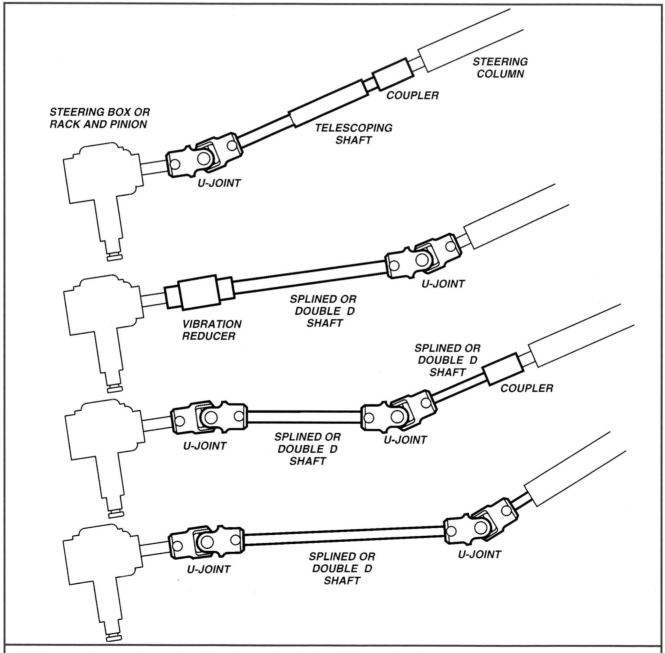

STEERING COLUMN

COUPLER

STEERING BOX OR RACK AND PINION

TELESCOPING SHAFT

U-JOINT

U-JOINT

VIBRATION REDUCER

SPLINED OR DOUBLE D SHAFT

SPLINED OR DOUBLE D SHAFT

COUPLER

U-JOINT

SPLINED OR DOUBLE D SHAFT

U-JOINT

U-JOINT

SPLINED OR DOUBLE D SHAFT

U-JOINT

This diagram shows typical configurations for steering shafts, U-joints, and various other components. Borgeson Universal

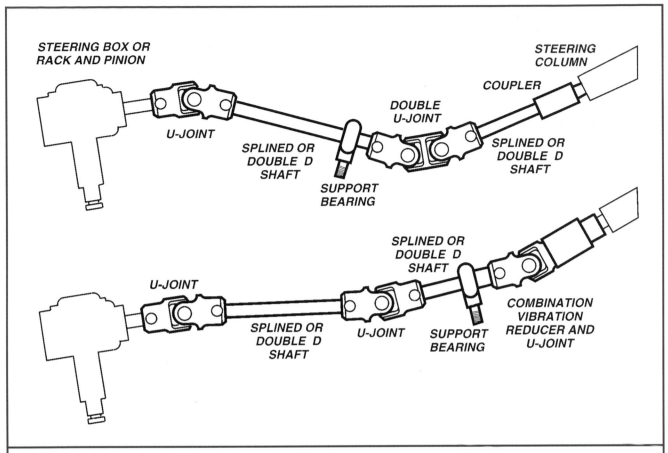

STEERING BOX OR
RACK AND PINION

STEERING
COLUMN

COUPLER

U-JOINT

DOUBLE
U-JOINT

SPLINED OR
DOUBLE D
SHAFT

SUPPORT
BEARING

SPLINED OR
DOUBLE D
SHAFT

U-JOINT

SPLINED OR
DOUBLE D
SHAFT

SPLINED OR
DOUBLE D
SHAFT

U-JOINT

SUPPORT
BEARING

COMBINATION
VIBRATION
REDUCER AND
U-JOINT

Any time more than three U-joints are used in a steering system (or drive shaft layout), a support bearing must be used to prevent looping and binding. Borgeson Universal

to a support hidden behind the dash. However it is done, the steering column must be secure.

One way to mock-up a steering column and wheel is to attach a round piece of cardboard to the end of a dowel rod. Make the cardboard the same approximate size as the steering wheel you plan to use. Slide into the seat and move the mock-up around until you find a position that feels most comfortable. This will give you an idea of what length steering column and column drop to buy or build.

Accelerator, brake, and clutch pedals

All pedals in the car need to be easily accessible and must not be placed in front of one another. In a fat-fendered rod, this is not a problem, but pedals can get crowded in a hurry in an early car, such as a Model A. The accelerator pedal is the most important in a hot rod, so it should be placed in a position that is comfortable for the driver for extended periods. There usually a flexible cable between the throttle and the pedal, so placement can vary somewhat.

Location of the brake pedal is pretty much determined by the master cylinder. Verify that your feet won't be caught

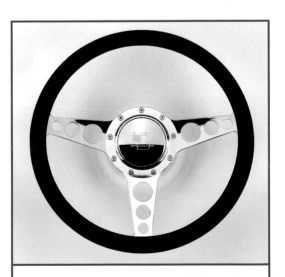

Billet Specialties offers a variety of steering wheels to match or complement its wheels. This GT half-wrap wheel is available in leather in a variety of colors to match your interior. Billet Specialties

89

These basic air conditioning components will be inside the car. The evaporator typically is placed behind the dash. Vents and defroster ducts can be placed wherever you want the cool (or warm) air, as long as you can route the hose from the evaporator to the vent. Also shown is the HVAC control panel, the supplied mounting brackets, and an expansion valve.

These basic air conditioning components are typically placed outside of the passenger compartment. The condenser is typically mounted in front of the radiator, while the compressor is mounted to the engine. A service port and binary switch are placed in line. The bulkhead is where the lines inside the passenger compartment are connected to the lines outside the passenger compartment. The drier can be mounted most anywhere, although it must be mounted upright and should be located in a relatively cool area of the car. A sample of fittings and hose are shown also.

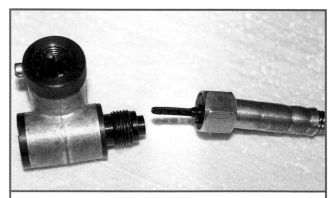

When using a mechanical speedometer, clearance for the sender cable directly behind the speedometer may be minimal. Using a 90-degree adapter will usually fix that problem.

Digital gauges and panels are available for common applications, such as this 1934 Ford, or for purely custom applications. Dakota Digital

Sometimes dash space doesn't allow for an extra gauge, so a steering column-mounted tach is a viable solution.

between the accelerator and brake pedals and that there is enough room to press one while not pressing the other at the same time. (And you wondered why automotive engineers made so much money.)

If your master cylinder is mounted beneath the floor, the brake pedal will extend up through the floor, thus requiring an opening. This opening will need to be shaped and sized so that movement of the brake pedal is not restricted by the floor, yet without leaving a gaping hole. What many rodders do is cut an oversized hole out of the floor to allow for service access to the master cylinder, as brake fluid will need to be added on occasion. Using some thin cardboard to make a pattern, an access cover is cut out of sheet metal and attached to the floor with self-tapping

screws. The access cover will need to have a slot cut in it that is wide enough never to rub on the brake pedal and long enough to offer sufficient pedal travel.

Adding a clutch pedal to the above mix is one reason that so many hot rods run automatic transmissions. Although it is not reason enough to avoid putting a manual tranny into a hot rod, considerable planning must be done to fit another pedal into the floorboard of many early cars. For this reason, it's good to have your pedals on hand in the mock-up stage so that you can ensure they will all fit with the spacing you desire. Depending on the location of the clutch pedal (if

91

In addition to the stereo, this console houses some switches and a map light.

used), access to its slave cylinder and floor clearance issues are comparable to those for a brake pedal.

HVAC unit

The evaporator portion of the HVAC system will usually be located between the dash and the firewall. What size unit to use will vary depending on the size of the vehicle you are using it in. The evaporator will need to be mounted securely, which may mean fabricating your own brackets. It will need to be mounted so that it does not conflict with gauges, the speedometer cable, throttle linkage, wiper motor, or anything else that is behind the dash. You must also allow room for the a/c, heat, and defrost ducts to reach their destinations, as well as coolant lines to the compressor.

In addition to the evaporator, there is a compressor, a condenser, and a drier to locate somewhere. The compressor is typically mounted on the engine and is belt-driven. The condenser can be built into the radiator, or can be a separate item attached to the radiator. If you know that you are going to be installing an a/c system, it is wise to use a radiator that has the condenser built in. The drier can be mounted almost anywhere; however, it is a critical part of the overall system, so it cannot be left out.

Gauges

Gauges are flexible in their location, so long as they are easily visible. About the only restriction is the sending unit for mechanical gauges, such as the speedometer. The speedometer cable cannot be kinked, so the path between the transmission and the back of the speedometer must follow a curvaceous route. A right-angle adaptor is available to connect the cable to the back of a mechanical speedometer. This may be a simple solution to the problem of not having enough room between the back of the speedometer and the a/c evaporator. This right-angle adaptor can also be equipped with a gear to correct the speedometer if necessary. Using electrical gauges can avoid some of the potential problems that mechanical senders might pose.

Stereo

If you rarely change the station or the volume on your stereo, it can go almost anywhere. On the other hand, if you are constantly changing stations, tapes, or CDs, the stereo should at least be within arm's reach and your peripheral vision. Besides in the center of the dash, a stereo can be mounted in an overhead or floor console, in the glove box, or even under the seat.

OUT IN THE GARAGE
Installing the HVAC unit

For a look at the basics of installing an air conditioning system, we contacted Keith Moritz at Morfab Customs. Without getting into a lengthy discussion of how air conditioning actually works, a quick overview is in order. Moisture in the a/c system changes from a liquid to a gas and then back to a liquid. The compressor (mounted on the engine and driven by the crankshaft) pumps refrigerant gas into the condenser. Heat is carried away from the gas at the condenser, thus condensing the gas into liquid. This liquid then flows into the dryer, then through the expansion valve where it is regulated, and then into the evaporator. While in the evaporator, the liquid absorbs heat (becoming a gas) and is then transferred back to the compressor to repeat the cycle.

One of Morfab's customers was installing air conditioning in a 1932 Ford coupe. This is what we found at the garage of Jan Schmelz.

1 The Vintage Air evaporator unit has already been installed behind the dash. Some mounting brackets are included with the unit; however, you should realize that it may be necessary to fabricate additional brackets depending on your application.

2 All air conditioning hoses will pass through the firewall by way of this bulkhead fitting (looking out from the inside). Note the use of foil-backed insulation. Don't make your a/c work any harder than it has to be.

3

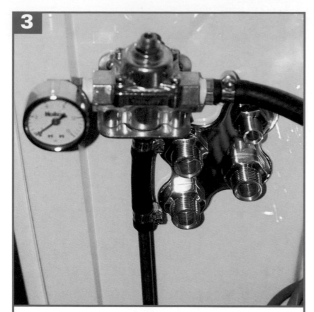

From the outside, we see the same clover-shaped bulkhead fitting prior to any hoses being connected. Two of these connections will be for the a/c lines, while the other two will be for the heater hoses. Note that the fitting with the hoses and the gauge is part of the fuel delivery system, not part of the a/c system.

4

Located in front of the radiator is the condenser. The grille shell has been moved during installation. The two fittings from the passenger side of the condenser will be plumbed into the system. The top fitting will receive refrigerant pumped from the compressor. The lower fitting will connect to the dryer.

5

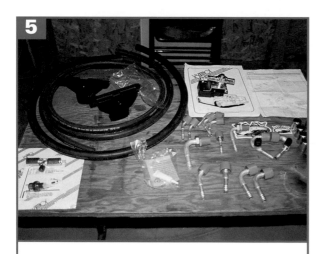

5 Some of the components not yet installed are the defrost vents and the hoses. A variety of fittings with different bends are available to make the routing of your hoses easier.

6 A pattern for the lower dash extension has been made. It will hide the evaporator and serve as a mounting location for three vents, the a/c controls, and a stereo.

6

7 The a/c compressor is driven by a belt from the crankshaft. Two fittings on the compressor are for high-pressure lines. One will feed refrigerant to the condenser mounted in front of the radiator. The other will receive a low pressure line from the evaporator.

8 Do not remove the caps from the compressor until you are ready to make the connections. Fittings are placed onto the compressor to establish the best routing and length of hoses.

9 With both fittings tightened onto the compressor, the hose can be routed to the appropriate connection and then cut to length. Air conditioning hose can be routed easily by simply twisting and turning it from one location to the next; however, it tends to remember that shape. For that reason, the fittings, ferrules, and hose should be marked with references so that the fittings will line up appropriately when installed for the final time in your hot rod. The hoses, ferrules, and fittings can now be crimped. (Note: Air conditioning lines are under extreme pressure and should therefore be crimped by a certified a/c technician.)
10 Before Keith makes any crimps, he lubes the hose.

11

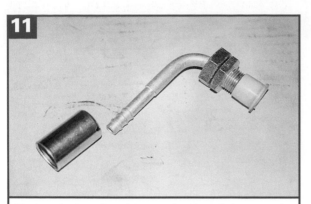

The hose is then slipped into the ferrule and then onto the barbed end of the appropriate fitting.

12

The hose simply slides into the ferrule until it bottoms out.

13

The hose and ferrule are then slid onto the barbed end of the fitting until past the barbs. This is probably the worst part of the crimping process and is usually tougher on the smaller hoses.

14

With the hose on the fitting, the ferrule is placed into the jaws of this crimping vise, which is simply mounted in a bench vise for use.

15

Using a wrench, the crimping vise is tightened to provide a uniform crimp.

16

A finished crimp that should not leak and therefore provide good service to your a/c system. (Note: When actually connecting the hoses for the final time, be sure to lube them, install O-rings, and tighten securely to avoid any leaks in the system.)

RUST REPAIR

One of the most popular reasons to purchase a fiberglass body for your hot rod project is that it won't rust. However, not all body styles are available in fiberglass, and there is still some good original tin out there. When dealing with a steel body, you will probably have some rust to deal with. This rust repair is not insurmountable (if it is, you would have passed on this particular project, right?), but it must be dealt with.

Typically, rust is going to be located in the lower portions of the vehicle. How high on the body the rust goes depends on how deep the car was sitting in the mud, dirt, and who knows what else before you rescued it. It is very common to replace door bottoms, cowl panels, rocker panels, and floorboards due to rust.

Patch panels

Whether you have the ability and equipment to do it yourself or not, patch panels should be welded in place, the metal worked as close as possible to the correct shape and then smoothed in with body filler as necessary to finish the job. In no case should a patch panel be held in place with just body filler or fiberglass. Don't laugh—I've seen it done.

Some patches can be done with fiberglass (using matte, cloth, and resin); however, having a steel patch panel welded in place is the better choice for steel-bodied hot rods.

For common hot rod bodies (read that as Ford), many patch panels are available from a variety of sources. Some are better than others, so check with other hot rodders to get their recommendations before ordering new panels. If the area to be repaired includes an intricate body line, a commercially available patch panel may be a necessity, while you may be able to fabricate your own simple panel, such as a door bottom patch.

Floor

Rust is also very common in floorboards and trunk floor pans. Because of this, don't be afraid to pull up an edge of the floor carpeting or move a spare tire around some when checking out a potential hot rod project. More than one vehicle has had some bodywork done and a new paint job applied to the outside bulk of the body without any regard for the rusty floor.

Just because there is some rust in the floor does not mean you should pass on a project, but a solid floor does go in the good column when it comes to building a hot rod. Several replacement panels are available (again, predominately for

Although these two swap meet items appear to be covered with rust, they are savable. Complete disassembly, a trip to Redi-Strip, and some epoxy primer would go a long way toward making them more eye-appealing.

97

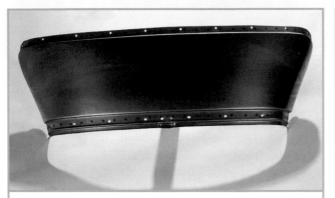

For popular models, most patch panels are available commercially. This filled cowl, along with a variety of other steel replacement panels for Fords. is available from Brookville Roadsters. Brookville Roadsters

This is a look at the door portion of a rotary latch in place. The female portion of the latch is usually placed in the moving part of the assembly, but not always. The release arm seen through the round hole will be attached to the door handle mechanism by a cable or rod, or it may be actuated electronically, depending on the application.

Ford products), but the aftermarket is growing. Of course, with some sheet metal and a welder, you can make your own replacement floor panels. Taking the time to make a good pattern will result in a better job. In addition to the actual sheet metal portion of the floor, you may need to make repairs to the subrails or other subfloor assemblies.

MODIFICATIONS (MILD)

There is almost no limit to the number or types of modifications that can be made to a hot rod. What too many rodders attempt to do, though, is modify something simply to change it. There is no reason for this. The importance of modifying something is to *improve* upon it. Perhaps a subtle difference, but an important one.

Door latches

A very common modification to contemporary hot rods is to eliminate the stock door latches. This is one area of hot rod building where the builder's creativity and imagination will come in handy. As long as the doors open and shut easily and lock and unlock at the proper times, how you make it all work is up to you. With the wide variety of original door latch mechanisms combined with remote entry systems and electric solenoids, properly secured doors along with the smooth look of no exterior door latches are easily obtainable. Faulty door latches are both an aggravation and a safety hazard, so take some time to get this often overlooked detail taken care of early on in your rod building project.

Although some rodders are still using stock-type door latches, a popular modification is to use rotary latches (commonly referred to as "bear claw" latches). These rotary latches are the same type as what is used in most new vehicles, so they provide a much safer latch. Consisting of two basic parts, a striker pin and a latch that wraps

around it, these latches are a vast improvement over most stock configurations.

Since rotary latches are not the same as stock, their use will necessitate some modifications to the door and doorjamb. For this reason, the actual latch mechanism should be installed early on in the building process.

Chopped top

Chopping a top in its most basic form means to lower the overall height of a vehicle by removing material from the window area. This requires removing material from the door and window posts, as well as from the actual glass.

With the excess window area in a stock Ford Model T or Model A, the proportions of the vehicle can be greatly improved by chopping the top. Chopping the top on a 1940 Ford coupe, on the other hand, usually does not improve the proportions. The amount of the chop is critical as well. Three inches out of the top of a Model A is about right, while six inches is about right on a 1951 Chevy wagon. Let moderation be your guide, as too much is usually worse than not enough.

Chopped tops are certainly not limited to hot rod coupes. More work is involved with a larger rod, such as this four-door sedan, but it's a great improvement.

This Model A Tudor has had a 3-inch top chop and a filled roof, greatly improving its looks over the original configuration.

Chopping the top on a Model T, Model A, or any other vehicle with near perfectly vertical door and window pillars is extremely simple, as long as you can weld decently. Determine how much to remove, cut that much out, and then weld the top back on. That is oversimplifying the process a bit, but not much. On the other hand, any vehicle that has windshield posts and/or doorposts that are not vertical will require a more significant amount of work to perform a decent top chop. The top will need to be enlarged or the windshield posts leaned back to rejoin the two components. Depending on the vehicle, the top may need to be stretched front to back or side to side or both.

No one method is a definite winner over another. It depends greatly on the style and purpose of the vehicle when it is finished. Raked-back windshield posts will give more of a competition look, while stretching the top may provide better proportions. Ask different people with vehicles similar to yours how the top was chopped before you cut up yours. A stock-height roof looks much better than a botched top chop.

Although this Model A Tudor uses nicer material than stock, it features a stock-style roof. Wooden bows span the opening in the top of the car. Material is then stretched across the opening and held in place with trim strips.

Filled roof

Many people do not even realize that a roof has been filled if they are not familiar with old cars. In the days prior to World War II, technology was not advanced enough to stamp a vehicle top as is common today. For that reason, most vehicle roofs had some wooden pieces spanning a large opening in the roof. To these wooden supports, some wire mesh and fabric would be attached, providing possibly the first "vinyl" roof. Filling the roof will provide more of a contemporary look to the vehicle, as well as eliminate the potential for leaks.

Again, depending on your vehicle, the source for roof filler material will vary. You will need to match the length, the width, and the curve (if any) of the existing roofline. Station wagon roofs were once popular for filler material; however, those are getting rare now. More abundant and lighter in weight are a whole new generation of minivans, SUVs, and extended cab pickups from which to scavenge material.

Filled cowl

Filling the common cowl vent should be done only if you are installing air conditioning, and not necessarily then. The cowl vent is a simple but very effective way of making the inside temperature of the vehicle similar to the outside temperature. If it is hot outside, it will be hot inside, but it will at least be fresh air. As most hot rods don't have vent windows, think twice before you fill that vent. The drawback of a cowl vent is that sometimes the mechanism will interfere with available room for installing an air conditioning unit. With some ingenuity, you can work around this if it becomes a problem.

Filling the cowl vent is usually done simply by welding the vent door in place and removing the opening mechanism. Body filler is then used to smooth the surrounding area. If the hood is peaked, remember to peak the cowl area to match.

Although the vent is mostly closed in this photo, it provides a shot of an operable cowl vent. When open, the cowl vent would typically stick up about 2 inches in the front.

The rear of this 1946 Ford has been given the smooth treatment. The bumper has been removed, the bumper bracket holes filled, and the pan rolled underneath.

Rolled pan

Creating a rolled pan involves removing the front or rear bumper and then rolling the exposed gravel pan under the body of the vehicle. Since rolled pans are commonly available as new replacement panels, it is often more cost effective to replace the existing pan than to actually modify it. If you are planning on running without bumpers, rolling the pan will help finish the vehicle.

Bumper smoothing

Another way to smooth the look of a vehicle yet retain the bumpers is to smooth them. If you can weld, you can do this in a weekend for a simple modification. Different people have their own process of doing this, but the basic approach is to tack-weld the bumper bolts to the outside of the bumper with the bumper in place. Then remove the bumper from the vehicle, slip a large flat washer over each bolt, and solidly weld the washer to the bolt and to the inside of the bumper. Adding this flat washer to each bolt will prevent the bolt from pulling through and leaving a square dent in the finished front surface of the bumper. When welding is completed, grind off the bolt heads from the outside of the bumper. Final finishing will vary somewhat, depending on whether you choose to have the bumper rechromed or painted.

MODIFICATIONS (WILD)

The following modifications are certainly not for the faint of heart and should probably be left to professionals. Made popular during the 1950s by customizers, these processes typically involve the entire vehicle; however, the same concept can be used on various portions of a vehicle for subtle modifications.

Channeling

Channeling refers to removing the floor from the vehicle, dropping the body down over the frame to a lower-than-stock location, then reinstalling the floor above the frame rails. This results in a lower-than-stock overall height while also eliminating some legroom in the vehicle. For some people this is not a problem, while for others it would be a major hindrance. Some reproduction bodies are designed to be channeled over the frame so that the floor pan fits between the frame rails and sits about as low as before, without losing as much legroom as would be lost if a steel body was channeled the same depth but in the traditional manner. Some channeling jobs lower the front of the body approximately an inch or two over the frame while leaving the back of the body in its stock location. This is usually done on highboy coupes to provide a more aggressive stance.

A subtle channel job may be a couple of inches or possibly the depth of the frame rails, while anything more may be extreme. Depending on the depth of the channel, it may also be necessary to modify the doors, as not so much of the door opening will be usable.

Sectioning

Sectioning removes height from the vehicle, much like a top chop; however, in this case the material is removed from the actual body of the car. This is perhaps the biggest of all body modifications, as you have to be committed to finishing this task once you start. No turning back after you have cut the top half off the car. By the very nature of this modification, it is more commonly found on newer slab-sided customs than on shapely hot rods.

Sectioning does have its place on hot rods, however. On fat-fendered hot rods, it may be desirable to section the hood. Often this is done by removing a wedge section from the sides of the hood, causing the hood to slope lower in front instead of riding flat. Sectioning can also be done to taillight stanchions, headlight stalks, and a variety of other pieces to pull them in closer to the body for a smoother appearance.

Suicide doors

I cannot imagine what automotive designers and advertising executives called doors that were hinged on the rear side when they were introduced. But it's hard to believe that salesmen pitching a 1933 Ford coupe used the term "suicide doors." Yes, that is the stock configuration straight from the factory.

There are several theories as to how they got this name. One theory is that because the doors created special dangers, people who bought cars with them were called suicidal, a name that transferred to the doors. Another is that gangsters who threw people out of them used suicide as an explanation for why they flew from the car. (But how did they explain the bullet holes?) Whatever the reason,

It appears that the bumper has been smoothed on this convertible. The things that you don't see (absence of bumper bolts in this case) are the details that lead to great hot rods.

This Mopar sedan features "rear-hinged" or "suicide" doors from the factory. It should be readily apparent that a faulty door latch could lead to severe damage to the body and door, and danger to the occupants.

several types of vehicles do feature this door-hinge setup in their stock configuration, while many others have been modified to have it.

Although they make a bigger door opening, suicide doors also create special risks. First, when they open during travel, the force of the air blows them *wide* open, creating a risk that someone will be ejected from the car—not to mention the damage it will do to your car. This has happened too many times to ignore the danger. A second risk arises when the car is stopped: If a passing vehicle strikes the door while you're standing between it and the car, it will smash the door into you, rather than knocking it open and probably off its hinges as with a regular door. If you use suicide doors, please be sure to install modern rotary-style latches.

Rotary latches (commonly known as "bear claw" latches), are a vast improvement over most of the stock door latches originally found in hot rods. Rotary latches are the same type that have been used by the automobile industry for over 40 years, so you know they must be safe.

These latches were originally installed in this Show Me Rod & Custom 1932 Ford roadster body, before it was delivered to Morfab Customs. The photos will provide a simplified version of the typical installation, as retrofitting them into a steel body will be more labor intensive, depending on your particular application.

1

The rotary latch assembly is made up of a striker pin and the latch with its release mechanism. Depending on installation, moving the release mechanism up or down will release the pin.

2

The necessary area is cut out of the door and the doorjamb. Be sure to maintain structural integrity, even if it means adding a structural support.

3

Use a piece of masking tape or a scribed line to indicate the striker pin alignment. Using the line to position each portion of the latch, drill the appropriate mounting holes in the door and the doorjamb.

4

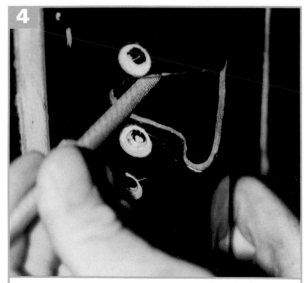

Some minor filing may be necessary to smooth out the opening for the latch. On fiberglass, a rat-tail file works great.

BODYWORK, REPAIR, AND MODIFICATIONS

5

The latch is then fitted into position . . .

6

. . . and secured in place with three screws.

7

The hole drilled for the striker pin required some minor filing too. The mounting pin of the striker pin is installed through the doorjamb and secured from behind with a lock nut (or nut and lock washer).

8

With the door hinged properly and the rotary latch properly installed, the door will close and latch easily and stay that way.

Installing a firewall

This Model A coupe is a hot rod from the 1960s that is ready for an update. Several chassis modifications, body repairs, and a general redo are in the works, including the installation of a new firewall. Follow along as we recap the process.

1

Drill out the spot rivets securing the old firewall to the cowl.

2

Before the firewall can be removed, this front toe board extension must be removed from the inside of the firewall to gain access to bolts securing the firewall to the frame.

3

Placing the fuel tank between the firewall and the passenger compartment was not one of Ford's better ideas. The fuel tank is therefore cut out. Make sure it is empty first.

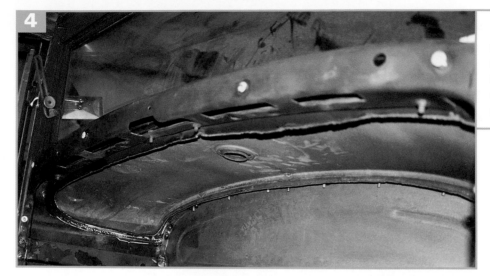

4 This is what the area behind the dash looks like with the fuel tank removed. Be sure to smooth up any rough sheet metal edges to avoid problems later on.

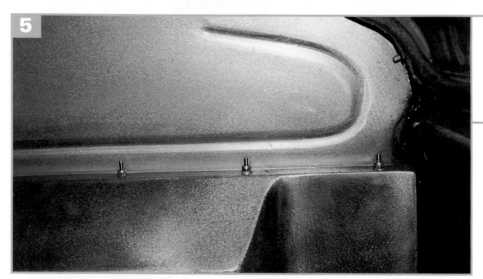

5 The Bitchin' Products firewall is a two-piece unit that is bolted together. With both pieces secured with bolts and lock nuts, it is positioned between the cowl panels.

6 In place, this is what the firewall looks like from inside.

7

When the new firewall is accurately positioned, it is spot-welded to the cowl . . .

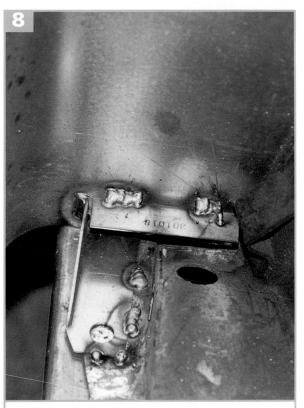

8

. . . and to the toe board extensions at the floor.

9

This is what the completed installation looks like from the outside.

10

From the inside, we see that new subrails and a new floorboard may be among the next things installed.

Chopping a top, filling the roof, and installing a delivery door

The author's 1929 Model A Tudor sedan on these pages will receive a mild top chop of 3 inches, combined with the installation of a rear delivery door and a filled roof. Gibbon Fiberglass Reproductions makes a kit to convert a standard Model A Tudor sedan into the much rarer sedan delivery. On the stock Tudor, the portion of the body above the beltline is a separate piece from the lower portion. New fiberglass panels for the sides along with a rear delivery door and jamb easily convert a Tudor into a sedan delivery.

When chopping the top and filling the roof, you chop the top first. This makes it easier to lift the top off the body simply because it will be lighter. Also, some massaging of the top will be necessary to fit it back on the car, which is easier to do before any welding stresses have been induced. A rear delivery door is also going to be installed to provide easy access to the rear of the vehicle. The kit is available in stock height or chopped 3 inches. We went with the 3 inches because this chop greatly improves the proportions of the Model A. It is very important to know for sure how much it has been chopped so that you can aim toward that same amount. This same 3 inches must be removed from the rest of the car for the top chop to work correctly. It could be that the actual measurement is 2-7/8 or maybe 3-1/8 inch, but as long as we match it, it doesn't really matter.

A simple procedure borrowed from the collision repair industry can make an easy chop even better. Many different methods have been used in the past to hammer the lids on Model As. However, the method used on this sedan seems to greatly simplify the procedure and will provide a stronger body. Instead of simply discarding the material removed (3 inches in this case), it was trimmed and used as a backing plate when the top was welded back on. This backing material is plug welded to the lower portion of the body. It greatly aids in aligning the top when it is reinstalled and then plug welded to the top. The seam between the top and bottom is then welded also. This all makes for a very strong modification.

In this particular Model A project, a sedan delivery door will be installed to facilitate easier access to the rear of the vehicle. However, instead of replacing the upper quarter panels with the solid delivery panels, the stock window opening will be retained, with the window glass in a fixed position. This will be done for a few different reasons. Several Model A sedans have been given the delivery treatment, so the windows are a slightly different approach to a now common modification. The windows will also make visibility a little better.

The body is securely mounted to the frame and supported on jack stands, ready for surgery.

2

With the known amount of chop in the delivery door, the amount to be cut is marked on the windshield pillars, door pillars, and rear quarters. Since this is going to be a 3-inch chop, two pieces of 1-1/2-inch-wide masking tape are butted alongside each other across the aforementioned vertical sections of the car.

3

Using an air saw or plasma cutter, the top is removed first by cutting along the upper tape line. The 3-inch pieces are then removed by cutting along the lower tape line but are not discarded. It is suggested you cut the top off first so that you don't have to chase the top around the shop floor trying to cut the 3-inch pieces from it.

4

After cutting the right rear quarter, the "B" pillar on the passenger side is cut.

Work progresses around the front of the car.

Finally, back around to the left rear quarter panel.

The top is then lifted off and set aside.

The 3-inch pieces then need to be cut from the lower portion of the body but not discarded.

9

Holes are drilled along the top of the lower panel of the body for the plug welds. The backing panel will extend down into the body approximately 1-1/2 inches, so these holes should be approximately 3/4-inch from the top edge.

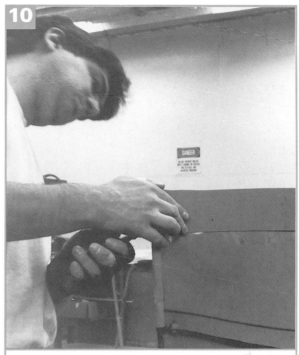

10

The 3-inch backing panel is now fitted into position and clamped in place.

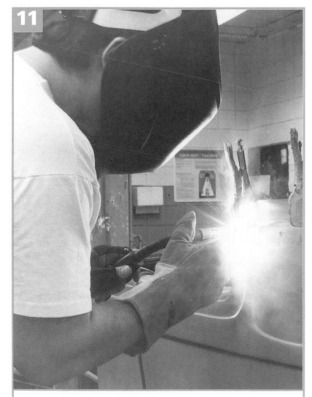

11

The backing panel is now plug-welded in place.

12

Holes are drilled in the lower posts. The pieces cut out of the doors and door pillars are then inserted into the lower posts. They will require some slicing to fit inside. The pillar inserts are then plug-welded into place.

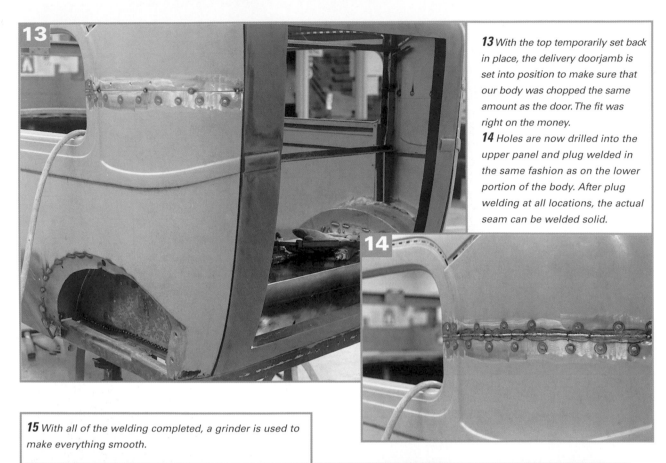

13 With the top temporarily set back in place, the delivery doorjamb is set into position to make sure that our body was chopped the same amount as the door. The fit was right on the money.

14 Holes are now drilled into the upper panel and plug welded in the same fashion as on the lower portion of the body. After plug welding at all locations, the actual seam can be welded solid.

15 With all of the welding completed, a grinder is used to make everything smooth.

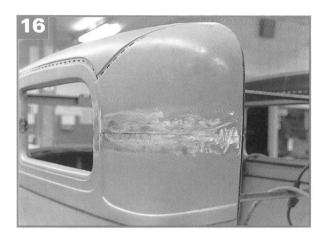

16 *A slight seam is visible, but a skim coat of body filler and some block sanding will take care of that.*

17 *With the top chopped, the doorjamb for the delivery door can be installed. It should be correctly positioned and clamped in place. Then the doorjamb and the rear panels of the sedan are drilled. The doorjamb then simply bolts into place. If you were simply replacing this middle section with a replacement steel panel, welding it in place would be a practical alternative. Since fiberglass cannot be welded to steel, this panel will be bolted in place and then caulked, leaving the characteristic body line in place, although the stock T-molding will not be used.*

18 *Now that the top is chopped, matching the delivery door height, the doors may be chopped to match. Bear in mind that a Model A (or T) has vertical door pillars, so corrections on a chop are relatively easy to make, while on a later-model vehicle, a slight mistake can ruin a project. After you bring the top down to the predetermined height, you should then cut the doors and make them fit the opening before welding them back together. Again, with the Model As having vertical pillars and also parallel top and bottom window lines, this is not so big a deal as it would be on a car such as a 1936 Ford coupe. The top of the door on a car like the 1936 Ford is not parallel to the bottom, so matching the angle of the top to the door frame would be much more difficult than matching the two sections of the door.*

The lower portion of the door is mounted, hinge pins installed, and the door clamped shut.

The top of the door is then hinged and the cutting point marked.

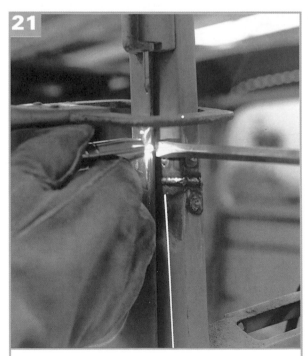

After cutting, the upper portion of the door is clamped into place and then welded back on to the lower portion. Make sure you don't weld the door shut.

After tack-welding the doors from the outside, they can be opened and welded on the inside as well.

23

Except for the inside garnish moldings, the chop is complete, greatly improving the proportions of this Model A.

24 The Tudor sedan on these pages will be covered with a roof from a mid-1960s Chevrolet station wagon. Not that that is the absolute best donor, but it was available. With a world full of minivans and SUVs, a new source of top filling material exists.

25 Since sheet metal cannot be welded to fiberglass (the delivery doorjamb), this epoxy from Lord-Fusor is used to glue the pieces together.

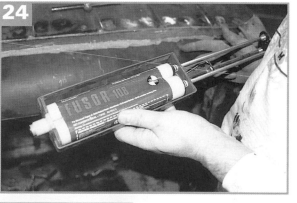

24

25

26

Where sheet metal abuts other sheet metal, the two pieces will later be welded together. Now, the epoxy is inserted between the sheet metal roof panel and the fiberglass doorjamb.

27

The top is then clamped into place. Small bolts are inserted through the top material . . .

28

. . . and then tightened from inside the car. The epoxy is then allowed to sit for the proper curing time.

29

With the epoxy cured, the top welded in place, and the welds ground down, the filled roof is finished with a small amount of body filler.

CHAPTER 5
PAINT PREP AND FINAL COLOR

Any good paint person or any textbook on the subject will tell you that the most important part of a high-quality paint job is surface preparation. Want to know why that is? Because it's the truth, plain and simple. High-quality paint products and application are very important, but surface preparation is the key to a superior finish. A paper-thin coat of paint is not going to smooth out a rough fender or straighten a wavy door panel. All too often, that is what people expect. A quick and dirty paint job may look good for a while; however, it will not last.

A fancy downdraft spray booth, top-of-the-line HVLP spray gun, and thousand-dollar-per-gallon paint is not going to straighten a wavy or dented panel. Those things may make your job easier if the panel is already arrow straight and smooth as glass, but not until then. A great friend of mine, who shall remain anonymous, has been painting hot rods and motorcycles since he was fourteen years old (and he is the same age as my mom). Vehicles that he has painted have won countless awards, been in the top running for Goodguys Custom of the Year Award several times, and been in more magazines than anyone cares to remember. His spray booth is merely a one-car bay in his concrete-block garage. He'll probably never use an HVLP spray gun. He knows how to use the old-fashioned gun that he's been using for a long time

A high-quality conventional spray gun will last a long time, as long as it is kept clean. With the advent of HVLP spray guns, conventional guns are now less expensive. By the time you prime and paint a complete hot rod or two, the savings in material cost (less overspray) will save the difference, however.

now. To paraphrase the wine commercial, he'll spray paint only when the bodywork is done.

Whether by panel replacement, chemical stripping, or media blasting, all rust should be eliminated from your hot rod before proceeding with the paint process. New paint will simply become a feeding ground for existing rust that is not removed.

Body panels that are not straight will not suddenly appear straight simply because of a new coat of paint. Likewise, sanding scratches will not disappear beneath a coat of paint either. In all actuality, a coat of glossy paint or sometimes even a new coat of primer will show that you have more bodywork to do than you thought.

Some colors are more forgiving to the bodyperson/painter than other colors. Usually, the darker the color, or the glossier the surface, the more easily poor bodywork will show through. The brighter the color, or the less glossy the surface, the more forgiving is the paint. If you plan to use a special-effect paint, such as pearl, candy, or metallic, each adds its own set of potential problems.

If you are doing the work on your hot rod yourself, and your metalworking skills are lacking, a bright yellow or

High-volume, low-pressure (HVLP) spray guns are designed to apply more material to the component being painted by spraying it at a lower pressure. This causes less material to bounce off and go into the atmosphere. At right is a full-size spray gun, while the smaller gun on the left is a "detail" or "touch-up" gun.

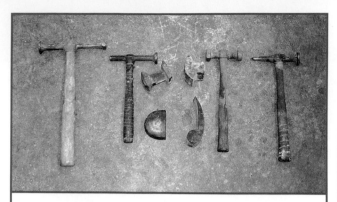

An assortment of body hammers and dollies is necessary if you are straightening, repairing, and otherwise saving an original tin body.

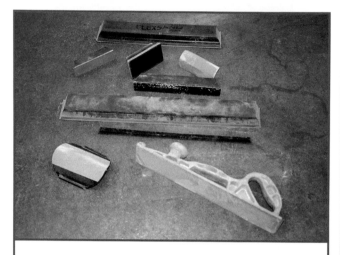

Whether you are resurrecting a steel-bodied car or attempting perfect paint on a fiberglass body, a variety of sanding boards and blocks will be necessary. Use the largest board or block available to get the straightest results.

this goes back to determining in the very beginning what you want to do with your hot rod. If you want it to be a daily beater, that's fine as long as the entire vehicle is built with that in mind. If you want it to be an over-the-top show vehicle, that's fine too, as long as all work is done to the same degree of craftsmanship.

When you choose a color for a hot rod, it should be a color that you like, not just one that may or may not hide problems. If the bodywork is as good as possible, the surface preparation is performed correctly, and a high-quality paint (in a color that you like) is applied according to the paint manufacturer's instructions, a paint job can last a long time. So why paint a vehicle in a color that may be popular today, ugly tomorrow, and completely outdated a month from now?

What color should you paint your hot rod? There are at least a half dozen basic colors of epoxy-based primer available from automotive paint suppliers. Most of those can be tinted by adding various amounts of toner. Most computer monitors are capable of seeing and reading 256 different colors, so I'll presume that toner is probably available in at least half that many colors. That gives us 128 different colors of toner that can be added to any of those six or more colors of epoxy primer. That's 768 different colors of primer and we haven't even thought about custom mixing any paint yet. So you tell the guy behind the counter that you want some red paint and you can't understand why he gives you a funny look?

History has proven that red, black, and yellow will always be popular with rodders. An old saying among rodders is that if you want to sell it, paint it red; if you want

Go to the paint store and tell the person behind the counter that you want a gallon of red paint. These are just two pages of a fleet color book. Very subtle differences, but all considered to be red.

orange may be a better choice than black or navy blue. However, the paint on your hot rod does not have to be perfect, so don't get stressed out about it. Your less-than-perfect paint might not win awards at the local car show, but with the money you save by doing it yourself, you can buy more material to practice with for that next rod project. By painting at least one vehicle yourself, you will be more understanding when you get that estimate from the painter on your next hot rod. If you drive your hot rod, you are eventually going to get rock chips and bug guts all over it anyway. Why do you think you see so many primered hot rods at events? Those are the guys who enjoy an event the most.

I enjoy and appreciate a finely painted hot rod as much as anybody, but you need to establish a realistic limit for paint work just like the rest of the work on the car. Again,

If you are going to paint a hot rod black, it needs to be as straight and smooth as possible, as black will show every flaw. Some subtle graphics such as on this 1933 Ford Victoria (Vicky) make it stand out.

to keep it, paint it black. Setting aside any preconceived notions about favorite colors, let's take a look at good and bad points of these popular colors.

Red (in its many shades and hues) is typically the best for catching someone's attention. If two otherwise identical hot rods were sitting next to each other, the red one will attract more attention than one painted any other color. If you want to stand out in a small group, red is the color for you. However, at a major rod run, that same red will start to become overwhelming, as so many rodders have the same thoughts that you do. As you might expect, most red paints are at the higher end of the price scale.

On a supersmooth, slick hot rod with perfect bodywork, nothing shows off that high quality like black. However, anything less than perfect should not be painted black, as the ultimate of dark colors will show every flaw or imperfection. Although it might take someone a second look to notice, the blackest black will garner its due attention if the prep work deserves it.

Another drawback of black is its reaction to high temperature. Consider using premium insulation and lots of it in your hot rod if you plan to be comfortable while driving in the sun. It should also be noted than several fiberglass manufacturers suggest not painting their products black. Since fiberglass involves a chemical reaction, high heat in combination with black paint may cause bodywork problems somewhere down the line.

Rounding out the top three most popular colors for hot rods must be yellow. It has many of the same good qualities as red: It stands out in a crowd, is fairly easy to keep clean, and photographs easily. Being lighter in color than most reds, yellow tends to be more forgiving of less-than-perfect bodywork. Some shades of yellow look better than others,

so do some looking before you make a final decision. Many shades of yellow attract bugs, however, so if you participate in a lot of events where your hot rod would be parked in the grass, you may want to choose a different color.

The color of a hot rod is certainly not limited to red, black, or yellow. These are just the primary colors that have remained popular over the long run. Any color you like is the color your hot rod should be. When choosing a color, look for something you won't quickly grow tired of, and try to avoid something that is trendy. What may look great today may be out of style sooner than you think (and before you can justify the need to repaint your hot rod).

The color on this roadster is from a Nissan pickup truck and isn't flashy; however, this car will have a crowd around it all weekend at a rod run. The light tan color is easy to keep clean and has stood the test of time for almost a decade.

While driving around town or sitting in traffic, look at vehicles around you. What colors do you see plenty of, which ones turn you head, which ones turn your stomach? More than likely, they will have the same effect on a hot rod as they do on a late-model vehicle.

CHASSIS

Chassis components (unlike lightweight body panels) can be "colorized" in a couple ways. First, there is the traditional method of painting, which is the same as painting the body. Second, there is powder coating, which provides a more durable finish, making it ideal for the underside of your hot rod.

Powder coating

The various components to be powder coated are hung from a hanger in a spray booth and connected to an electrical charge, where they are coated with colored powder. This electric charge is what draws the powder to the parts and pieces being coated. The coated pieces are then placed in an oven where the powder essentially melts onto the assembly. Different formulations of powder, higher or lower temperatures, and longer or shorter baking times yield different characteristics in the finished product. Among these are gloss, texture, durability, and corrosion resistance.

A limiting factor to the use of powder coating is that the coated material must be able to withstand the oven temperature of approximately 500 degrees Fahrenheit. Therefore, no plastic body filler may be used to repair or customize the part to be coated. Any imperfections must be filled with lead or a metal patch welded in place. Prior to having a part powder coated, it must first be cleaned to bare metal, either by chemical stripping, media blasting, or sanding.

Powder coating has both advantages and disadvantages when compared to paint. Powder coating is more durable than most paint in that it resists flaking. A powder-coated piece may sustain a small chip but will not flake off like paint does at times. Powder coating is also able to withstand exposure to most chemicals (gasoline, oil, etc.) that it may encounter.

On the downside is the fact that powder coating can be expensive. Since powder coating requires specialized equipment (mainly the spray gun, a booth, and an oven), it is usually done by companies who are subcontractors for factories who manufacture a large volume of similar pieces. They are not going to be able to coat your chassis bright red while in the middle of a production run of 10,000 semiglossy purple widgets. The company in question may be able to give you what you want, but it will usually be according to their schedule and not yours. Even if the powder coater is ready to coat your parts, an oven big enough to do your parts may not be available. If their bread-and-butter business is coating foot-long widgets, they most likely will not have a baking facility large enough to properly cure a chassis.

With the increased popularity of this process among hot rodders, powder-coating facilities that cater more to hot rodders are becoming more common. Even if your local powder coater does not have the ability to cure a complete frame, it may be desirable to have any of a number of smaller chassis components powder coated. Using neutral or contrasting colors adjacent to the painted frame rails works well to detail your chassis. The master cylinder, four-link bars, brake drums, and wheels are all items that could benefit from the durability of powder coating.

Paint

Whether you are painting the chassis, body, or whatever, it is a good idea to use components from the same company throughout the project. No one paint manufacturer has the absolute best product for all of the different circumstances you may encounter when building a hot rod. However, with all of the testing that is done for their products, any one company is going to be able to tell you what is the best base surface for their product, as well as what is best to apply over it. Simply put, there is no need for you, the rod builder, to play chemist. Pick a brand based on whatever you want to base it on, whether that is local availability, cost, or advertising.

If you are painting the chassis, you will typically be using the same products and methods that are used on the body of the car. The good part about this is that you will be partially familiar with the product, simply because at least some primer has probably already been applied to the body by this time. A wider range of colors is available in paint form than in powder coating. This will generally make matching or complementing your final body color easier. Paint can also be touched up, while powder coating typically cannot.

Sanding

If you have decided to paint your chassis, the first item that must be attended to (after any necessary structural or functional modifications, of course) is surface preparation. Depending on the intended use of your hot rod, a little or a lot of work can be involved here. Some rodders may choose simply to prime and paint the chassis, while others will completely smooth it to the same degree that the body is finished. The chassis will obviously not be seen as much as the body, so if you don't plan to do extensive sanding throughout your hot rod, save it for the body. A nicely detailed chassis is something to be proud of, however.

The following procedure will give the basic rundown for paint prep for a chassis using the basecoat/clearcoat system that is widely accepted as the norm. For this purpose, it is presumed that the chassis is free from rust. This same procedure will apply to all of the chassis components, the frame, suspension components, axles, etc.

The paint products listed are from PPG; however, similar products are available from other companies.

Priming and sealing

Situate the chassis so that all parts of it are accessible to be painted. Ideally, this will be low enough so that you can paint one side of it easily, yet high enough that you can paint the other side fairly easily also. Remember that the front frame rails are typically going to be seen when viewing the engine (from above), while the rear of the frame will typically be seen only from below after the body is installed.

The next step is to clean the chassis with DX330 Wax and Grease Remover. This is typically applied to a clean towel and then wiped over the surface. Another clean towel is then used to wipe off the surface, keeping the DX330 from drying on the surface. The chassis can now be sanded with 180- or 220-grit sandpaper.

Using an air nozzle, remove any sanding residue from the surface. Verify that dust, dirt, or sanding residue is also blown out of any cracks or crevices. The chassis can now be primed with DP Epoxy LF, which is available in approximately six different colors, including black, gray, and brown (hot rod red). The procedure thus far would also be appropriate for priming parts upon delivery (well in advance of being ready for paint) to avoid rust forming on them if your shop is not adequately climate controlled.

Now is the time to finish any bodywork that needs to be completed. This may include boxing any brackets that have not yet been done, as well as any general smoothing that is desired. By following the directions, any of the high-quality plastic fillers now available can be used to achieve professional-looking results on your chassis. Another coat of DP Epoxy LF should now be applied. The DP Epoxy LF is nonporous (unlike most single-part primers), which makes it resistant to moisture that would cause problems later on. The LF designation simply means that the primer is lead free.

A filler primer such as K36 (mixed as a surfacer) should now be applied. Just like the epoxy primer previously, as well as any subsequent coats, all primer, surfacers, sealers, basecoats, and clearcoats should be stirred properly prior to mixing to make up for settling. Mixing with the appropriate reducers or catalysts should be done according to the directions for existing shop temperature, proper number of coats applied, and proper drying times allowed. Be sure to use the appropriate air-supply volume for your spray gun. Note that conventional and HVLP guns have different air requirements.

After allowing the proper drying time for sanding, the chassis can now be wet sanded using 400- or 600-grit sandpaper depending on the color and type of paint. A finer grit (600) should be used for darker colors or metallics, while a coarser grit (400) should be used for lighter colors or solids. Obviously, the finer grit could be used with lighter colors or solids as well; however, it is not necessary.

Prior to applying any paint, the primer and surfacer layers of the chassis and components should be sealed. Either K36 or K93 should be mixed as a sealer and applied. A definite plus about using either of these products is that they may be tinted. Why would you want to tint the sealer, since you are going to paint right over it? If you have tinted the primer (the same color as the component to be painted), rock chips and other "to the primer" damage is less noticeable. One of the differences in these two products is their final appearance. The K36 provides more of an eggshell appearance, while the K93 looks much like the finished paint, except that it is about one shade from the true color when tinted.

Painting

DBC basecoat in the color of your choice can now be applied. Normally, two to three coats will be adequate; however, lighter colors may require more coats to achieve complete coverage. Higher-quality paint jobs will have additional coats of color. As long as there are no runs, drips, or other mistakes in the basecoat, it is not necessary to sand it. If there are mistakes that need to be sanded out, additional coats of basecoat must be applied to the sanded areas to achieve the proper coverage.

Two or three coats of DCU2002 can now be applied. If you plan to sand and buff the chassis, three or four coats of clear would be appropriate. Additional coats of clear may be sprayed and sanded for a higher-quality finish. The main concept to remember with basecoat/clearcoat is to achieve coverage with the basecoat. It is perfectly normal for the basecoat to look dull; however, the clear is not going to cover anything that the basecoat does not. The application of the clearcoat is what will supply the gloss.

BODY COMPONENTS

Now that you have successfully painted the chassis (or found someone else's work that you approve of), the body and other components can be painted. It should be mentioned that all bodywork should be finished before the chassis is powder coated or painted. You for sure don't want to be slinging body filler or dripping primer all over a completely finished chassis.

A special note about fiberglass bodies and fenders

Due to the chemical reaction required in their construction, fiberglass components must be allowed to cure. Bodies and fenders (or any other fiberglass component) should be mounted to the chassis (using the proper bolts, shims, etc.) as soon as possible after purchasing them. The fiberglass pieces should then be scuffed with 80-grit sandpaper and allowed to sit in the sun (preferably the summer sun) for as long as possible before doing the final block sanding in

The Paint Store recommends Evercoat "Rage Gold" body filler. Like all other body fillers, it must be mixed with hardener in the appropriate ratio to work properly.

Sanding material is available in a variety of types and grits. Long strips are for use with sanding boards, sheets are for use with a variety of sanding blocks, and discs are for use with orbital sanders.

preparation for painting. This scuffing allows the fiberglass to breathe, while the heat from the sun allows the fiberglass to cure.

If the curing procedure takes place while those new fenders are merely leaning against your workbench, their fit with your hot rod body may not be as good as you had hoped. If you go to the trouble of block sanding the new fiberglass pieces and then they continue to move around while in the curing process, you have wasted a lot of time and effort.

Bodywork

By this time, bodywork should be limited to disassembling the body to prepare it for paint. Disassembling the various assemblies as completely as possible will provide the best results, although this will add to the required time. Be sure to label and store any pieces that will not be painted (such as chrome trim or rubber weather stripping) in a safe location.

Sanding

Now break out the sandpaper, sanding boards, and sanding blocks. As much as you may be inclined, don't allow just anyone to sand on your hot rod. Sure, anyone can do it, but not everybody will do it correctly. The general tendency for the uninitiated is to sand in one relatively small area at a time. This results in a smooth divot in the panel being sanded.

The proper method for sanding is to use as long of a sanding board or block as possible and to move it in an overlapping "X" pattern. This allows you to smooth the entire panel instead of just part of it. Whether you are using a regular sanding block or a scrap piece of 2x4, use

Adequate lighting, plenty of working space, proper ventilation, and appropriate protection from chemicals are extremely important when painting a hot rod. Hanging the components or resting them on a sturdy support within your reach is also important.

something more than just your fingertips to back the sanding paper. If not, you will end up with grooves approximately the size of your fingertips in your hot rod's body.

Primer/sealer

The next step is to clean the body components with DX330 Wax and Grease Remover, just as you did the chassis. Using an air nozzle, remove any sanding residue from the surface. Verify that dust, dirt, or sanding residue is also blown out of any cracks or crevices. Go over the entire car several times to make sure you get all of the debris blown out.

The body can now be primed with DP Epoxy LF in your favorite shade (or maybe the shade closest to your final color choice). When the primer is dry, thoroughly inspect all body panels and look for any blemishes. Any necessary body filler (should be very minor amounts at this point) can be applied on top of the epoxy primer. If you did not use epoxy primer, it will be necessary to grind back down to bare metal to achieve a good bond. When the filler has cured, another coat of DP Epoxy LF should be applied and block sanded with 280-grit paper.

A filler primer such as K36 (mixed as a surfacer) should now be applied and wet sanded using 400-grit sandpaper after the proper curing time. Now apply K36 or K93 (mixed as a sealer and tinted if desired) and allow to dry before wet sanding with 600-grit sandpaper.

Color

You may now begin spraying your favorite color of DBC basecoat. Like on the chassis, two or three coats will be adequate; however, lighter colors may require more coats to achieve complete coverage. When you are finished applying the color coats, you can begin spraying the clear, such as 2021 Clearcoat. Two or three coats of clear will be sufficient and should then be sanded and polished.

If you desire a glass-like appearance, spray three coats of clear and then sand flat with 800-grit paper. Now apply two more coats of clear, then sand with 1000, 1500, and finally 2000 grit. Polish, buff, and then apply your favorite liquid or paste wax.

OUT IN THE GARAGE
Installing a third brake light (or flush mount tail lights)

The following procedure shows how a third brake light was installed above the delivery door of the author's Model A sedan. Larger taillights could be installed in the same way.

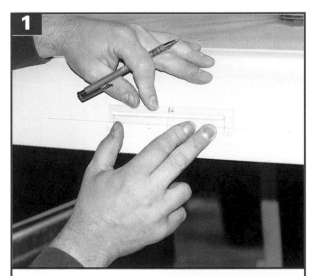

Another task that should be completed prior to painting is installing the third brake light, if it will require any bodywork. After marking a baseline above the upper lip of the delivery door and locating the center from side to side, the outline of the brake light is marked on the body.

The actual lens portion of the brake light is translucent, so it is somewhat difficult to see against the light-colored primer. With the flat part of the light mounted from the inside of the body, the lens portion protrudes through an opening that will be cut in the body. The lens can then be sanded down to match the contour of the body.

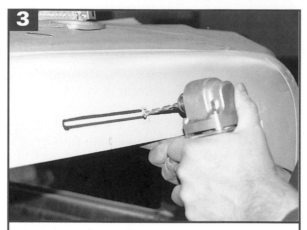

After marking the location for the third brake light, a drill is used to form the round ends of the hole through which it will protrude.

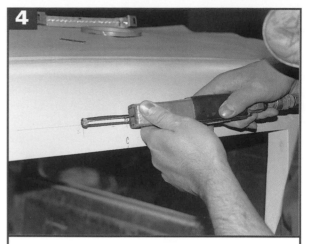

Using a pneumatic saw, the body material is cut away for the light.

A die grinder with as large a disc as possible is then used to true up the edges of the opening.

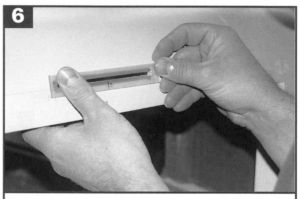

This piece of the taillight will actually be mounted from the inside; however, it can be checked for fit from the outside.

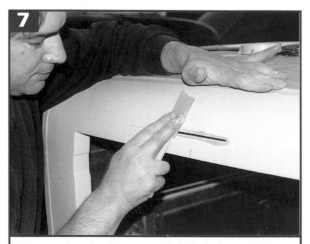

Using a paint stir stick as a sanding block, the primer is sanded away from the opening for the third brake light.

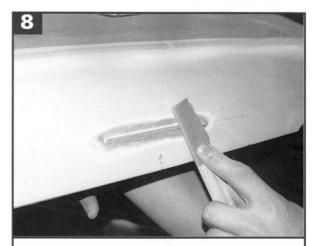

With the lens in position from inside the body, a piece of sandpaper wrapped around a paint stir stick shapes the lens to conform to the shape of the body.

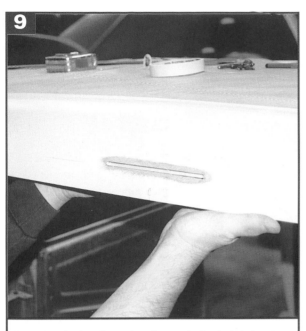

9

Now that the lens is conforming to the body, it is barely noticeable yet will provide plenty of brake light when needed.

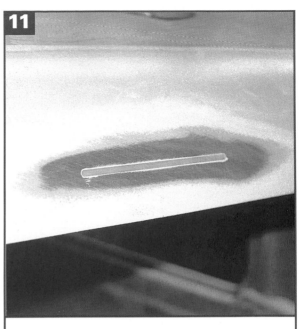

11

With the addition of the body filler and it then being sanded smooth, it appears that the hole was cut to the exact shape and size necessary.

10

To fill any imperfections that may have existed in the opening, a light skim coat of plastic body filler is spread over the light and the immediate area. After it dries, the filler is then sanded smooth.

CHASSIS

Now the real fun of building a hot rod begins—when you start assembling all of those painted, polished, plated pieces for what should be the last time. Although the pile of parts may look intimidating, it should be no problem to assemble them, because if you have followed well-intentioned advice, they have all been together already. Even though you may want to put the entire car together this week so that you can attend a rod run next weekend, resist that urge. You already have a fair amount of time and money invested in this project by this time, so don't botch that up by getting in a hurry now.

Although various subassemblies throughout your hot rod may already be together, it makes good sense to perform the final assembly of the chassis first. This will allow you greater access to many of these components and will make the bulk of the vehicle easier to move around that much sooner.

Front suspension assembly

Whether you are building a slender-fendered, fat-fendered, or no-fendered hot rod, a good place to start the final assembly of the chassis is with the front suspension. It doesn't matter if you are using a dropped front axle or independent suspension. Typically, there are more pieces and parts in the front suspension than the rear, so you will be closer to completion if you start here.

If you planned ahead and kept some decent notes during the preliminary mock-up, this assembly should go easily. You will already know how long each four-link needs to be or how many shims need to be on each side of the upper and lower control arms.

With the chassis securely and safely supported on jack stands, begin by laying out all of the suspension pieces near their intended location. The actual components will vary depending on if you are installing a dropped axle or an independent suspension, but now is the time to verify that you haven't misplaced anything. If you don't have one, buy, borrow, or rent a torque wrench. Make sure you have adequate chassis lube and several shop towels on hand as well. Some soft towels will come in handy to keep from scratching the paint or chrome on the pieces as they are assembled.

A double U-joint can be used to avoid excessive angles in the steering system. If these double U-joints are used in conjunction with one or more other U-joints, a support bearing must be used. Borgeson Universal

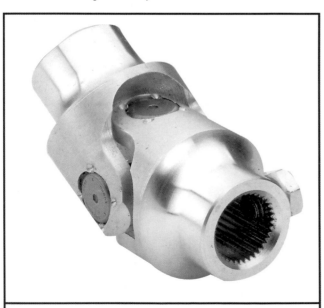

Most every hot rod is going to need at least one U-joint to connect the steering column to the steering box. This close-up shows the splines inside the joint. Borgeson Universal

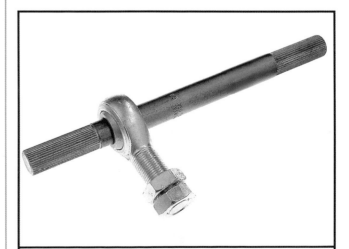

Any time more than two U-joints are used in a steering system, support bearings are required to prevent "looping" and binding. Borgeson Universal

This is a Heidt's Superide kit, installed in a Morfab Customs 1933–1934 Ford chassis. Realize that there is no weight of an engine or front sheet metal to compress the springs, thus the "lofty" stance.

Follow the instructions provided or your notes to assemble the front suspension. Make sure you follow torque specs, install lock nuts (or lock washers), and cotter pins (where required), and that the assembly moves as it should. Take the time to double-check that all nuts and bolts are tightened properly. Double-check that cotter pins (of adequate size) are installed.

Wheel bearings will need to be packed in grease as they are assembled; however, you may choose to wait until the entire assembly is together to lube the chassis. Just don't forget to do it sometime before that first drive.

Depending on what type of steering you are using (Vega box, rack and pinion, etc.) go ahead and hook up as much

of it now as possible. The final linkage to the steering column probably cannot be done until the body is installed, but it will be easier to get to now than later.

A common source of vibration, whether in a driveshaft or a steering shaft, is having the shaft "out of phase." The upper example shows the universal joints aligned properly, while the lower example shows an out-of-phase situation that will lead to vibration and possibly premature failure of the universal joints.

To avoid vibration and premature failure, steering shafts and drive shafts must be "in-phase." The top layout is correct, while the bottom layout is "out of phase." Borgeson Universal

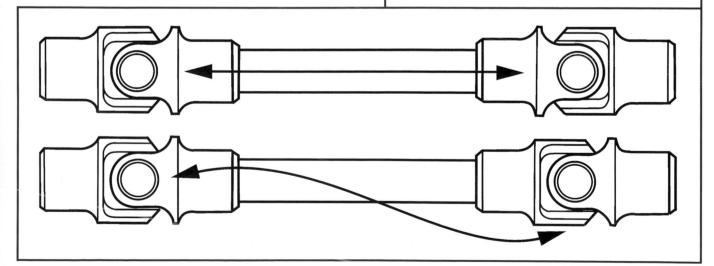

Check out the combination upper shock mount and headlight bracket on this chassis. Combining ideas to make one bracket serve multiple functions is part of the fun of building a hot rod.

Rear suspension assembly

Although the components are different, assembling the rear suspension is much like assembling the front. Make sure you have all of the pieces and the proper tools. It will be necessary to have a floor jack to lift the rear axle housing into position while installing the suspension components. Make sure the adjustable components are adjusted properly and that all fasteners are secure. Don't forget to add the proper lubrication to the differential. Don't laugh—that has been forgotten more than once. Make sure the pinion angle is set correctly as well. The pinion shaft should be positioned so that it is at the equal and opposite angle of the output shaft of the engine and transmission. Ideally, the output shaft of the tranny should be downward approximately 2 or 3 degrees, with the pinion shaft pointing upward the same amount, so that if imaginary lines were extended from them, the lines would be parallel when viewed from the side. The mounts for the rear suspension should be attached to the rear axle housing to provide this equal and opposite angle.

With all of the suspension components secured in place, you can now bolt on that set of wheels and tires. You *do* have the wheels mounted and balanced, don't you? If you don't have them balanced, do yourself a favor and have that done now, before you even bother bolting them on. If you are installing aluminum wheels, make sure you use some type of anti-seize lubricant to keep the lug nuts from welding themselves to the wheel studs. Use a torque wrench to verify that the wheel are tightened to the proper specs. This is especially important on aluminum wheels, and most manufacturers will suggest rechecking the torque after a certain number of miles. Make sure you do.

Now sit back, have a glass of lemonade, and seize the moment. You have now assembled a complete rolling chassis. Most of your work to this point will be covered up eventually, so feel free to pull out the Kodak and snap a few photos for the family album, or a digital camera so you can post the progress on your website.

Master cylinder/booster assembly and brake lines

Okay, finish the lemonade you have more work to do. The master cylinder and brake booster (if used) can now be bolted into place. Make sure it is securely fastened and not moving around. If you are using a brake booster, make sure you run a vacuum line to an appropriate source. Quite often this is on the back of the carburetor, which is not yet installed, but just don't forget it.

Ideally, you have already bent all of the brake lines. For some inexpensive detailing points, scuff OEM brake line with very fine steel wool, and then spray it with clear. This doesn't look quite as good as polished stainless brake lines, but it looks better than stock. Install all of your brake lines, check valves, proportioning valves, and any other brake line components you may have chosen. Verify that all connections are tightened. Use brake line clamps (available in a wide variety of styles and price ranges) to secure the brake line to the chassis. Except for flexible lines used to run to the wheels, none of the brake line should move. Any movement may eventually lead to rubbing, which could rub a small hole in the brake line. To prevent moisture from entering the system, fill the master cylinder with brake fluid and bleed the brakes. This is much easier to do now than when the body is on the car.

Engine and transmission

Whether you are using a new crate motor or a rebuilt engine, you will be ahead of the game if you get it dialed in and running as it should on a test stand before installing it

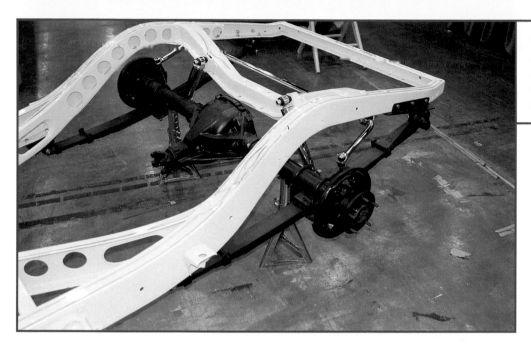

This photo gives a good overview of a parallel leaf spring suspension. Note the sway bar behind the rear axle.

in your hot rod. It is much easier to tune the engine if it is mounted to a test stand, connected to a *safe* fuel supply, and cooled by a proven radiator. This way, you are not dealing with trivial items such as clogged fuel filters, bad ignition wiring, or transmission or other drivetrain problems. Sure, the ultimate tuning can only be done with the hot rod as a whole, but if you know that the engine has been dialed in previously, that maiden voyage can be spent listening for other irregularities.

Before installing the engine in your hot rod, you should also install all of the miscellaneous items that may not be necessary for the engine to run on a test stand but that are necessary in a running automobile. This includes the starter, intake manifold, distributor, fuel pump, oil pressure sending unit, water temperature sending unit, transmission, and anything else that you can think of. Before you bolt up the transmission, be sure you have the thrust washer and pressure plate or torque converter in place. It is

Although this Morfab Customs chassis isn't actually painted, it does give a glimpse of what would be a milestone of the rod building process. With the addition of wheels and tires, this unpainted chassis is just about ready to be a roller.

The engine in this roadster is well detailed and very clean. Note the use of color along with polished components to add contrast to the engine. In this photographer's opinion, this theme looks much better than simply chroming everything.

much easier to install these items if you can actually see what you are doing and have enough room to use the correct tools. On some hot rods this may not be a problem, but on some it will be. Best to find out now so you can make any necessary changes.

Make sure that you use the correct bolts and that they are tightened to the proper specs and in the proper sequence.

Lower the engine and transmission into place while someone else guides the assembly into position. When it's in the correct position, install the cushion part of the motor mounts and transmission mounts, and then secure the engine and transmission on the chassis. Double-check that all mounting bolts are properly tightened. If using a shifter that mounts directly to the transmission, it should be installed at this time. Just remember to remove the tranny access cover(s) from the floor before positioning the body down over the protruding shifter.

Although the actual wiring will come later, relatively easy access would make this a good time to install the sending units for the water temperature and oil pressure gauges. Consult the installation instructions for your particular application for additional information. Now is the time to install belts, sparks plugs and wires, aftermarket valve covers, and any other engine components that are not currently in place. Finish the engine and transmission installation by checking and *verifying* that the engine oil and transmission fluid levels are to the appropriate marks on the appropriate dipsticks. Other than fuel, spark, and coolant, your engine should be ready to run by the time you finish this step.

EXHAUST

After the rolling chassis is fully assembled, but before the body goes on, it is a great time to have the exhaust installed. Without the body in the way, it will be much easier for the exhaust installer to do a nice job of routing the exhaust and do any necessary welding.

Radiator

Depending on the particular body style of the hot rod you are building, the installation of the radiator may need to be choreographed with the grille and fender installation. However, in most instances the radiator can be installed now. From your preliminary mock-up procedure and your notes, you should know exactly what has to be done. If you are using an electric fan mounted to the rear of the radiator, it may be a good idea to install it prior to having the radiator in the car. For maximum cooling efficiency and safety, be sure to install a fan shroud.

With the radiator in place, radiator hoses can be run to the engine. Don't forget to install the appropriate thermostat and correct mixture of coolant/antifreeze. Resist the urge to avoid using a funnel while pouring coolant into the radiator. Most antifreeze is not good for paint, plus it just plain makes a mess when it is spilled. If you do spill some antifreeze, be sure to wipe it up with a clean, dry shop towel as soon as possible. If possible, rinse the area with clean water to minimize any ill effects of antifreeze on painted or polished surfaces.

You should avoid spilling anything else, but especially brake fluid, on a painted surface. Although brake fluid is not quite as bad on the newer urethane paints as it is on older lacquers and enamels, it still isn't good for them. If brake fluid or any other hydraulic fluid is spilled on a painted surface, it should be soaked up, rather than wiped off, so quickly as possible. Wiping tends to spread the contaminant onto more surface area. Silicone brake fluid is supposed to be safe for paint; however, it is very expensive when compared to ordinary brake fluid and the two cannot be used in conjunction.

BODY

Most hot rod bodies will require mounting blocks and/or frame webbing to be installed between the frame and the body. The webbing is usually held in place with some type of adhesive included with the kit, or the webbing may have an adhesive backing while the body mount blocks are held in place by the weight of the body. A small bit of trim or weatherstripping adhesive on the body mount blocks will help keep them in position while you are maneuvering the body into place.

Main body

On an open car, it is best to leave the doors in place and latched to help keep the body from flexing. On a closed vehicle, the doors can be removed, as the body is less likely to flex simply because of its design. After verifying that the mounting blocks and webbing are in place, have as many of your biggest, strongest buddies you can gather come over and set the body in place. If you play it smart, you can pretend to check the location of everything while they do all the lifting. This depends greatly on the size/weight of the vehicle body and the size/strength of those doing the lifting. On a fiberglass track T, one average guy on each side could probably handle the chore with no problem. With the minute size of the car, many more guys would simply get

Many aftermarket headers and countless custom headers are available for engines of all makes. These block hugger–style headers are designed to sit close to the engine in order to fit between the frame rails of early cars.

Although hot rods usually don't get as many miles put on them as daily drivers, and the exhaust material is usually better, it may be necessary to remove the exhaust from your hot rod somewhere along the line. Plan ahead and use some bolt-together flanges rather than welding the complete system together. Also, make sure there is enough room between the rear axle housing and the exhaust.

in each other's way, thereby causing potential problems. On, say, a '48 Buick Roadmaster, the longer body would give more room for more hands to grab ahold of it. Whatever the vehicle, someone has to lift while one or possibly two people watch for alignment and interference. If you are using a hoist to move the body, you will need someone to operate the hoist, with at least two other people (one on each side or end) to assist in aligning the body with the frame. Since you have already had the body on and off the frame several times, you undoubtedly have the bolt holes drilled already. Use some alignment bars to get the holes lined up, then secure the body to the frame. Be sure to use sufficient body mount bolts and lock washers.

Fenders, splash aprons, and running boards

With the exception of Ford Model As (and possibly some other brand vehicles), the fenders, splash aprons, and running boards are installed after the body is on the chassis. On Model As, the front fenders and running board splash aprons are installed before the body goes on the chassis. A subtle difference perhaps, but certainly one worth noting if it applies to your vehicle.

Again, if you took the time to do the preliminary fitting prior to painting, fender installation should go smoothly and with a minor amount of touch-up required. If you did not take the time to do that, however, you will quickly

realize why you should have when you are working with painted pieces. Make sure you use the correct nuts, bolts, washers, and shims during the final assembly of the body components. Although all hardware needs to be tight, do not overtighten, as this can cause damage, especially in fiberglass components.

Fuel tank(s)

Depending on the location of your fuel tank, it is probably about time to install it if not done already. Verify that it is mounted securely, does not move, and is well vented. You will need to install the fuel gauge sender (don't forget to ground it) and run the fuel line to the fuel pump and then on to the carburetor. If your fuel tank requires a filler nozzle, install it now.

Doors

Now it's time to fit the doors. Take all the time necessary to make them fit just right. You'll want your door gaps— one of the main ways to tell a carefully built rod from a thrown-together one—to be even and the door surface to rest level with the body all the way around. Ill-fitting doors won't work right, they won't look good, and you'll risk scratching your beautiful paint on the door or body if they scuff together at a tight spot.

If you used shims to align the doors previously during mock-up, you will need to install them again. Verify that the doors open, close, and latch as you intend before you move on.

Hood and deck lid

The hood and deck lid are just more doors to make sure that you have installed correctly. If you had them to the point of working flawlessly while everything was in primer, they should work that well now that they are wearing finished paint. If not, you will begin to understand why you see many hot rods in primer. It's not that the builder doesn't want a painted car, it's simply a matter of the car not being ready for paint yet. I would much rather have a primered hot rod that works flawlessly than have a completely painted one that shows signs of ill-fitting panels.

Lights

That pile of parts out in the garage is starting to take some shape now, isn't it? To be able to obtain license plates for it, you have to put some lights on it. Lights may take away from the smoothness of the car at this point; however, you have to have them. During your planning and mock-up stages, the best location for headlights on your hot rod has already been determined. Bodywork is all done and everything is painted, so you might as well go with that original plan.

OUT IN THE GARAGE
Assembling a dropped axle front end

For the straight scoop on how to install a dropped axle front suspension, we checked with Keith Moritz at Morfab Customs. Keith was in the process of installing a four-link system on one of his 1932 Ford chassis. The assembly process is the same whether you are mocking up the suspension with unpainted parts or doing final assembly with finished pieces. About the only difference is that some additional care must be taken to avoid scratching paint.

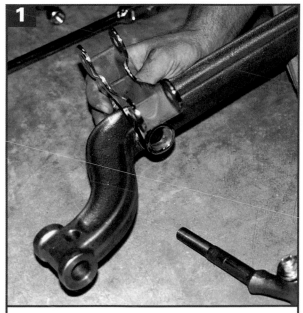

Start by sliding the batwing over the perch bosses of the front axle.

The transverse spring is connected to the spring perches with a shackle at each end. Slide one pin of the shackle through the spring eye and the other through the perch. Slide the shackle link onto the pins, and secure with two nuts. The spring can be mounted to the perches before or after the perches are installed in the axle. The threaded end of the spring perch slides through the top portion of the batwing, the axle, and then the lower portion of the batwing.

To secure the spring perch, the lower shock mount is slid on, and a nut is tightened onto the protruding threads of the spring perch.

4

With both spring perches and spring installed, the axle and spring assembly can be positioned under the front cross member of the chassis. A centering pin in the top leaf of the spring fits into a hole in the cross member. During this mock-up stage, Keith is installing only the main leaf. During final assembly, the additional spring leaves would be installed and secured to the main leaf with spring clamps. A monoleaf spring is installed in the same manner as a main leaf but does not require additional leaves.

5

The spring is now secured to the cross member with two U-bolts, a spring pad, and four lock nuts.

6

Since only the main leaf is installed, Keith temporarily installs a short bolt to act as a centering pin. If using a monoleaf spring, be sure to include the shims that make up the difference between the multileaf and monoleaf springs.

7

If locations for the frame brackets are included with the instructions for your particular kit, use them to position the frame brackets on the bottom of the frame rails. If location measurements are not included, thread the adjusters for the four-link half way into the bar. Mount the bars into the batwings, and then use the bars to determine the correct location for the brackets. Be sure to have adjustability in the four-link in order to align the vehicle.

8

After determining the location for the four-link frame brackets, Keith tack-welds them into place. It is best to tack-weld everything first and then assemble to make sure everything fits.

9

A drift or alignment bar may be necessary for lining up the four-link bar with the batwing to install the bolt.

10

After installing the front bolt in the top bar, the rear bolt is installed. Verify that the bolts are tightened securely with a lock nut.

11

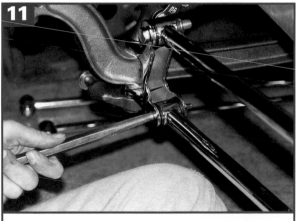

Again, an alignment tool may be necessary to line everything up.

12

Install the bolts and lock nuts on the lower bar.

13

With one side completed, Keith moves on to the other side to repeat the process. Note that the tack welding of the frame brackets should be completed on both sides prior to installing the bars.

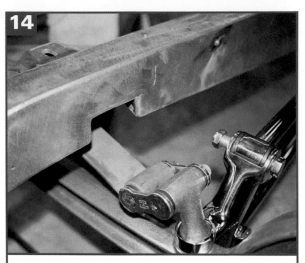

14

This close-up shows an optional notch that has been cut into the frame rails. It will provide extra clearance for the spring in this chassis. This notch has been fully boxed, so no strength is lost.

15

The lower end of the shocks will slide onto the lower shock mount below the axle and be secured with a lock nut. The upper end will mount to a frame bracket that will be installed later.

Engine detailing ideas: A photo gallery of nicely detailed engine compartments

Whether your hot rod is a down-and-dirty late-night street racer or a fairgrounds trailer queen, or somewhere in between, being a hot rod, its engine is going to be its primary focal spot. So whether it hauls or gets hauled, the engine needs to look good. Following are a variety of engines for you to check out.

1

The Ford flathead engine was once the mainstay of the hot rod movement. Even though they have been replaced in popularity by the Chevy small block, the flathead still looks great and is still number one in the hearts of many. Painted and highlighted heads match the block. A fair amount of sparkle highlights the color, while attention to detail makes it all look good.

2

If your hot rod is a black-with-flames Willys coupe, subtle just won't work when it comes to an engine. This rodder installed a big block, complete with a polished tunnel ram intake, and dual quad carbs, with most everything polished.

3

This primered roadster utilizes the popular Chevy small block for power. Highly polished components highlight the red block and inserts on the valve covers and air cleaner. Note the clean routing of the wiring.

4

No doubt about it, a lot of money was spent on this engine compartment. A RamJet Injected 502 big block with all chromed accessories sure does look good. Note the hard lines connected to the air conditioning compressor.

5

Note the use of hard lines at all possible locations in the plumbing of this small block. Be aware that hard line requires some flex line, thereby producing more connections.

6

Smooth the inside of the engine compartment, paint it to match the body, then install a well-detailed, blown fat block. Some brute horsepower with finesse.

7

It doesn't have to be a V-8 to be a hot rod. This little four-banger no doubt gets this roadster up to speed quite handily. Nothing fancy, but it doesn't require a second mortgage. Remember, it's the power-to-weight ratio that matters.

MECHANICAL COMPONENTS

Whether you have your hot rod all painted and are assembling it for the last time or are just getting it drivable, installing certain components in the interior is very important. You can do without stereo, air conditioning, and power windows (at least for a while). But you can't do without such things as the accelerator pedal, brake pedal (and clutch pedal if using a standard transmission), shifter linkage, and door handles that work properly. Although they should work properly when installed, you won't be the first hot rodder who doesn't have an operating emergency brake or window risers the first time you take your hot rod out for a drive.

Pedals

Accelerator pedal Aftermarket accelerator pedals typically come in two varieties. One type is mounted by

This hot rod in progress gives an example of some of the things that are seldom seen in a finished hot rod. Note the wiring from behind the dash, running down to the neutral safety switch located at the base of the shifter. Insulation is also used to minimize engine/exhaust heat and noise.

installing bolts (or screws) through the firewall directly into threaded holes in the pedal mounting bracket. The second type is mounted by installing bolts (or screws) through the firewall, through a mounting flange, and then secured with a locknut. If installed properly, either one will work correctly. However, on the first type, if the bolt becomes loose, it can easily strip out the threads in the pedal mounting bracket, rendering it useless. The flange type mount is probably easier to install, especially for the first-time builder.

When installing the accelerator pedal, verify that the pedal (and throttle linkage) will not overcenter that is, go beyond the point to where the cable or linkage would naturally return to idle if your foot was lifted from the accelerator pedal creating a wide-open throttle situation. Also, make sure that the movement of the pedal is comparable to the movement of the throttle linkage on the carburetor. On a typical aftermarket spoon-type accelerator pedal, the pedal is actually on a lower arm that is pushed downward by the driver. This causes an upper arm (adjustable in relationship to the lower arm) to pivot rearward, pulling on the throttle linkage via a cable or

This is the brake pedal arm passing through the firewall of a fiberglass 1932 Ford roadster. The hole must be large enough for the pedal arm to pass through during its entire travel.

rod. If the throttle linkage on the carburetor has a possible movement of 90 degrees (as an example), but the accelerator pedal is situated to travel only 45 degrees, you won't be able to get full acceleration. In all essence, you will have created a governor for your hot rod, and who would want that?

Brake pedal The brake pedal actually consists of two components—the pedal arm that pivots and is connected to the plunger in the master cylinder, and the brake pedal pad. Although you do not want a gaping hole around the pedal arm, there must be a sufficient clearance (in the floor) for the pedal arm to move through its necessary travel. It may be necessary to cut a larger than necessary hole in the floor to actually install and service the master cylinder and then bolt in filler panels to eliminate a major draft. Be sure to smooth the edges and round the corners on these filler panels to help minimize gouging the underside of the carpeting. The pedal arm must be able to move far enough to push the plunger fully into the master cylinder before actually being limited by the floorboard.

Depending on the available interior room in your hot rod (and the size of your feet), you may need to shop around for the ideal-size brake pedal pad. If the pad is too big, you may get your foot caught behind it when moving from accelerator to brake. If the pedal is too small, it may be easy to miss in a panic stop situation. Most aftermarket pedals are similar in size; however, some one-off pedals seen in the past were less than well thought out.

Clutch pedal If you're running a standard transmission, obviously you will need a clutch pedal. For aesthetics, you should choose one that is about the same size as the brake pedal. Not that a clutch pedal is big, but like everything else, it does take up some room, so plan ahead.

Shifter linkage Whether you are using a floor shifter or column-mounted shifter, make sure the linkage is adjusted correctly. Although it sounds silly, make sure the transmission is actually in the gear that the shifter indicates it is in. Verify that shifter mounting bolts are securely tightened. The transmission is absorbing all of the horsepower that your mega engine is producing, so any vibration will quickly loosen any bolts that aren't adequately tightened. Double-check to verify that movement of the shifter linkage is not restricted by contact with any part of the body or chassis or by the operation of the brake pedal; also verify that the shifter linkage does not rub against any wiring or plumbing lines.

Emergency brake

When installing the emergency brake, you must also install a foolproof way to disengage the emergency brake completely. Make sure that none of the linkages is binding and that no cables are rubbing on anything. An emergency brake release cable can be worn through rather quickly if not protected.

Window risers (mechanisms and handles)

Most problems associated with roll-up windows are due to the glass being the incorrect size. If the glass is too short (front to back), it will tend to rock back and forth and eventually bind. If the glass is too long (front to back), or if the window channel is not smooth, the glass will bind. With window glass being somewhat strong, something has to give if the glass is in a bind. This will usually be either the riser mechanism (inside the door) or the handle (the part you crank).

Stock window riser mechanisms and most reproduction pieces are assembled with rivets. If the glass gets into a bind, these rivets will shear. The originals if undamaged are reliable; however, there is a simple fix for new or old. Simply remove the window mechanism from the car, drill out the rivets, and replace them with appropriately sized bolts and lock nuts. Window handles are prone to stripping if they are not secured to the shaft and the glass gets into a bind.

Although aftermarket window mechanisms are available in both manual and electric, these OEM power units from a 1963 Buick Riviera are common enough in salvage yards, and they work well.

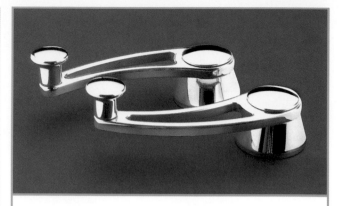

There is no reason that your interior should not look every bit as good as your engine compartment. These window risers are sure to dress up any interior. A collar is secured to the shaft of the window riser mechanism with set screws, then hidden with the aluminum cover. The arm is then secured to the collar in one of several different positions (allowing you to match your handles from side to side), and the cap is pressed into place, secured by an internal O-ring. Billet Specialties

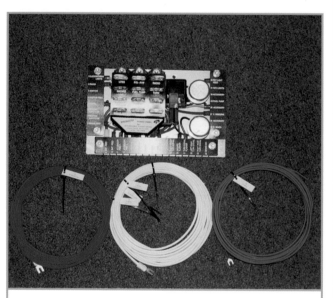

The Wiremaster fuse panel from Affordable Street Rods is a great place to start when wiring your hot rod. The compact panel requires only a small space, making it easy to install. The wires (many more than shown here) are all labeled as to what terminal they are to be connected to and where the opposite end is to be connected. Since the wires are all individual, you can run the wiring as needed or as time allows. In other words, you can run enough wires to get the car running and then later add the wiring for the a/c when you install those components.

Door latches and handles

Although some rodders are still using stock-type door latches, a popular modification is to use rotary latches (commonly referred to as "bear claw" latches). These rotary latches are the same type that is used in most new vehicles, so they provide a much safer latch. Consisting of two basic parts, a striker pin and a latch that wraps around it, these latches are a vast improvement over most stock configurations.

Since rotary latches are not the same as stock, their use will necessitate some modifications to the door and doorjamb. For this reason, the actual latch mechanism should be installed early on in the building process.

It is easy to utilize stock (or repro) door handles even with rotary latches. Depending on the actual vehicle, you may need to do some thinking about the latch mechanism to make sure that it does not interfere with the up-and-down movement of the door glass. On some vehicles, it may be necessary to install the larger latch mechanism in the doorjamb and the smaller striker pin in the door. In this instance, it may be necessary to use remote-control power door locks.

ELECTRICAL COMPONENTS

The main thing you need to learn about electrical components is that they will not work properly if they are not grounded properly. They may work, but not accurately or consistently. Do yourself a favor and establish a good ground for all electrical components in your hot rod. This becomes more difficult in a fiberglass-bodied car, but it certainly can be done.

Running electrical wires through a moving panel, such as a door or deck lid, is just a problem waiting to happen. These electrical contacts can eliminate those ugly wires that are always in peril while hanging out in the doorjamb area. One contact is surface-mounted to the doorjamb on the hinged side, while its counterpart is mounted to the door. When the door is closed, the two will make contact. Dakota Digital

Using a heavy-duty battery cable (the same diameter as the positive battery cable), the battery should be grounded to the engine or transmission. The starter can be grounded to this same location or to a convenient location on the chassis. Don't be afraid to scrape the grounding area down to bare metal, and be sure to use a serrated washer to help maintain a good ground. All of the interior components could be grounded to a common location and then connected to a common grounded at the engine or chassis. Be sure to use a heavy enough wire to carry the load of the various components.

Another bit of wiring advice is to use a rubber grommet anytime that electrical wire passes through sheet metal. Without a grommet, the wire's insulation can easily be worn off, thus creating a short that could be difficult to find.

HVAC system

The air conditioning system is complex to install because of its various components and the space they take up. It requires a fair amount of electrical work as well. Studying the instructions included with your air conditioning system beforehand and making sure that you are familiar with the parts will make this job much easier.

Much of the required wiring is included with the air conditioning components and just has to be routed between them and connected. It will also be necessary to install a few electrical relays, so you should determine a secure mounting location for them that is also out of the way. The air conditioning system will require power from the fuse panel, as well as a good ground.

Gauges

Although they are not absolutely necessary, almost all hot rods have at least a few gauges. If you actually drive your hot rod, you should have a speedometer and a fuel level gauge. You don't want to be thrown in jail for speeding through Deadatnight, Ohio, and you for sure don't want to run out of gas there. A typical hot rod uses a volt gauge, a fuel level gauge, an oil pressure gauge, and a water temperature gauge, in addition to a speedometer and an optional tachometer.

If you are not one to watch gauges, you should at least install a warning light for the oil pressure and water temperature—which can tell you whether your expensive motor is in trouble before something expensive breaks. Since you are reading this, we will assume that you want to know how your hot rod is performing, making gauges a practical thing.

All gauges will vary somewhat in installation, so verify the proper installation with the instructions provided with them. For the most part, the gauges require three basic inputs. These are an electrical source to power the gauge (and lights), a signal input (mechanical or electrical), and a good ground. Electrical gauges are the standard setup today and are easy to install.

Typically, a signal to the voltmeter is through a wire directly to the fuse panel. This signal wire can then be

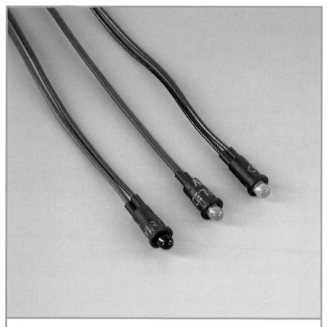

For turn signal indicator lights, high beam indicators, or a variety of other lighting tasks, these tiny lights provide a large amount of light for their size. Although they are available in different sizes, the smallest ones are usually more than adequate. Dakota Digital

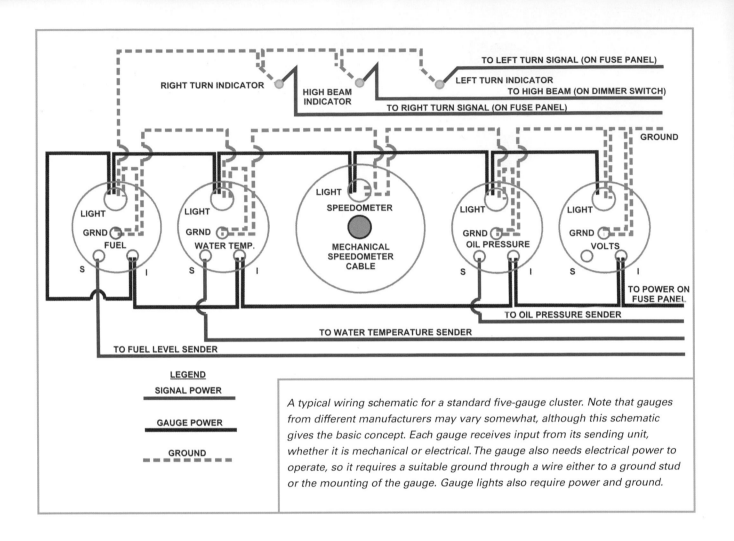

A typical wiring schematic for a standard five-gauge cluster. Note that gauges from different manufacturers may vary somewhat, although this schematic gives the basic concept. Each gauge receives input from its sending unit, whether it is mechanical or electrical. The gauge also needs electrical power to operate, so it requires a suitable ground through a wire either to a ground stud or the mounting of the gauge. Gauge lights also require power and ground.

jumped to the power terminals of each gauge. Depending on your gauges and your fuse panel, a separate wire may supply power to the lights of your gauges, or you may use the power source also.

The fuel level, temperature, and pressure gauges (and speedometer, if electric) are then connected to their respective senders to receive a signal input. Fuel level senders are generally located at the top of the fuel tank. Temperature senders are normally located on the intake manifold, while pressure sensors are usually located in the engine block. Provide a good ground to each gauge and you are in business.

A good practice that can make service easier in the future is to wire all of the gauges and terminate the wires with a quick disconnect. This allows you to wire the gauges on your workbench, instead of while standing on your head inside the vehicle. Be sure to leave enough slack in the wires so that you can remove a gauge from the dashboard before disconnecting it. This will spare you a lot of hassle if you have to repair a gauge.

Stereo, speakers, and amplifiers

When installing your stereo system, position it so that it can easily be operated while cruisin' down the street or highway. You shouldn't have to stretch or divert much of your attention away from driving just to listen to some tunes or the ballgame. The stock dash area of most hot rods is relatively small, so a console overhead or extending from below the dash may be necessary to house the receiver or CD player.

Speakers come in a wide variety of shapes and sizes (as well as prices), so finding something that will fit your hot rod should not be a problem. Speakers can be mounted to use the stock speaker grilles or recessed behind the upholstery (as long as the upholstery has holes in it). It may be a good idea to consult with your upholsterer before purchasing speakers, just to see if he or she has any particular recommendations for placement. A simple way to customize your stereo is to paint the speaker grilles the same (or a complementary) color as your upholstery material. In most cases, this will look better than the

Here's an example of a nice, clean, tasteful interior. Comfortable bucket seats covered with leather, sculptured door panels, and carpeting. Note the use of a polished stainless sill plate to protect the doorsill.

stock black speakers will. Try to avoid placing speakers in the doors, as the repeated movement can cause them to loosen from their mounts and will also cause excessive wear on the wires.

If using an amplifier, it should be mounted in a location that will have at least a minimal amount of air around it. This can be in an enclosed area, but it needs to be slightly larger than the amplifier itself. Make sure that the stereo and amplifier are properly grounded and that all related wires (yes, even speaker wires) pass through rubber grommets when routed through sheet metal.

Lights

Besides instrument lights, three other important lights should be mounted in the dash (the source of paradise illumination). These are the two turn signal indicators (please use them) and the high-beam indicator. Indica-

tor lights are available in a variety of colors and sizes, yet even the smallest will easily do the job.

Typically, all hot rods have a dome (or map) light. It may not be the coolest part of your hot rod, but if you ever need one, you'll be glad that you have it. Being relatively inexpensive and easy to install makes them a convenience that no one should be lacking. Simply mount the light and run a power wire to it from the fuse panel (and/or headlight switch, depending on your application), along with a ground wire, and that should be it.

Combination courtesy/marker lights can be installed (usually low) in the doors. These are usually split into two lenses, one white and one red, even though they come on at the same time. The white portion of the light serves as a courtesy light when getting in or out of the car. The red portion serves as a marker light to oncoming traffic that the door is open. As on a late-model vehicle, these lights are operated from a push-button switch located in the doorjamb. When the door is closed, the power circuit is open and the lights are off. When the door is opened, the switch closes the circuit and the lights come on.

WIRING

Wiring is one task in building a hot rod that in this writer's opinion the car owners should do themselves. Wiring is the central nervous system of the hot rod. If you are familiar with it, you will be better prepared to make a roadside repair, if necessary. Hot rods are generic enough that eventually someone will come along who knows what is wrong with the carburetor, fuel pump, or whatever, if your side-of-the-road predicament is mechanical in nature. If it is electrical, however, a decent memory of where each particular wire is routed through the car will make your wire-tracing job much easier.

A wide variety of fuse panels and wiring kits are available, so it is best to shop around before you plunk down your hard-earned cash. Most wiring kits are color coded, typically using GM color coding. Some kits are sold a la carte, so you are required to purchase more wiring for each electrical component that your hot rod uses. Other kits consist of a wiring harness that plugs into the fuse panel. The bad thing about this setup is that if a portion of the wiring harness goes bad, you may be required to rewire the entire vehicle.

Using a kit that uses a fuse panel with enough dedicated circuits for your hot rod, and separate wires for each of those circuits, is a practical way to go. Install the fuse panel and enough wires to make the engine run, and you can at least enjoy your hot rod in your own driveway. As you have time, you can wire the lights, stereo, etc., until you are finished. Although your hot rod may not get finished any sooner this way, you won't be so likely to get burned out on the wiring process.

Installing the fuse panel

Before installing your fuse panel, consider that you may actually have to install a new fuse at some time. Some out-of-the-way location that is easily accessible is ideal. Many late-model automobiles have moved the fuse panel from under the dash (very inconvenient) to the end of the padded dash (accessible from an open door). Depending on what kind of hot rod you are building, a console, kick panel, or trunk may be an acceptable location.

Wherever you mount the fuse panel, it should not move or be subject to repeated impact. Having sufficient room for wires to make sweeping turns, rather than sharp bends, will minimize stress on the terminal connections, as well as provide some air around the fuse panel.

Running wiring

Best advice for running wiring is to take your time, plan it out in your mind (or on paper), and have plenty of wire ties available so that you can enjoy the intimate experience with your hot rod. Begin by connecting the appropriate wire to the first terminal and then route it to the component it is to be connected to. Remember to use rubber grommets when passing wires through sheet metal or rough fiberglass. When you are satisfied with the routing, cut off any extra wire (leave yourself some slack), crimp on the appropriate terminal connector, and make the connection. Then loosely place a wire tie approximately every foot along this first wire.

From the next fuse panel terminal that supplies power to something in the vicinity of this first wire, connect the appropriate wire. Then run the wire through these loose wire ties until you have reached your destination. Repeat the process of cutting the wire, crimping on a terminal connector, and making the connection. When you have three or four strands of wire in your wire ties, they can be tightened and the excess tie cut off. If you have more wires to run along this same route, simply add more loose wire ties. You may also use wire ties to tie a bundle of wires to a support to help keep them from moving around.

SEATING AND UPHOLSTERY

The interior of your hot rod will say a lot about the overall style (and age) of the vehicle. It is easy enough to change wheels or even paint to change the exterior appearance of a hot rod. However, with the relative expense of upholstery and trim, the interior is usually not changed as often as the rest of the car may be. For this reason, consider conservative patterns, timeless materials, and neutral colors when designing an interior. Although wood dash panels are attempting to make a comeback, nothing says 1970 any more than an interior trimmed in red crushed velvet (with lots of buttons) and burled oak.

Real leather, although expensive, will always be in style as an interior material. A very nice alternative to leather is a product known as UltraLeather. Being easier for the upholsterer to work with and softer on your bottom (your wallet too, but only slightly), it's an impressive product. High-quality tweed (yes, there are different grades) when used in conservative colors will always look good too. When you are looking for material for your hot rod interior, think more along the lines of a comfortable family room rather than a formal sitting room.

When installing the seat(s), be sure to use Grade 8 fasteners. You do not want the seat to break loose from the car and to toss you about in the instance of a collision. Being secured by a seat belt into a seat that is adequately secured to the floor of your hot rod is the safest place to be if you are in an accident.

If you used shims to mock-up the seat location during your preliminary mock-up, use them now during final assembly as well. You are going to be spending a lot of time in the seat of your hot rod, so it needs to be positioned comfortably.

GLASS INSTALLATION

Unless you just happen to be well versed in the art of automotive glass installation, this is an area that is best left to the pros. Making an accurate pattern, cutting the glass, installing the glass, and making sure that it doesn't leak is more than beyond the hobby capabilities of most folks. Glass installers who know what they are doing make it look easy. Knowing the tricks of the trade make that happen; however, I don't recall ever being in a glass shop where there wasn't at least one guy missing one of his fingers.

Another reason to take your hot rod to a glass shop is that if they break the glass while installing it, they replace it. If you break it while installing it yourself, guess who pays for the replacement glass?

OUT IN THE GARAGE
Upholstering a door panel (or interior panel)

To find out how to do some upholstery work, we contacted Sam Wright Hot Rod Interiors. Although Sammy was working on a 1955 Chevrolet at the time of our visit, the same procedures would be used on a hot rod, a pickup truck, or a street machine.

The panel illustrated is for the right rear interior panel. When finished, the panel will be multilayered and covered with light tan UltraLeather material.

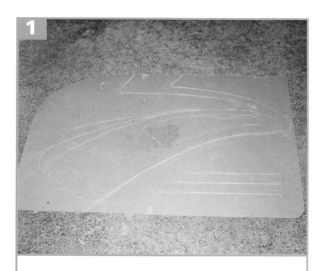

Using a piece of pattern paper (approximately 1/16-inch-thick tagboard), Sammy has already cut out a pattern that is the same size and shape as the area to be covered. Such items as holes for mounting clips, screws, etc., are located on this overall pattern. The design is also sketched onto the pattern.

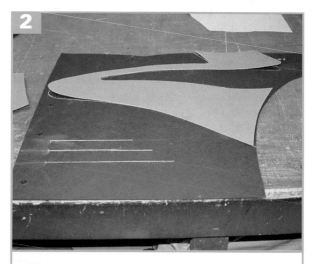

The design portion is cut out from the pattern paper and laid out onto panel board. (Panel board is approximately 1/8-inch thick. Some trimmers will use lauan plywood or preformed ABS panels.) The pattern is then traced around with chalk to transfer the pattern to the panel board.

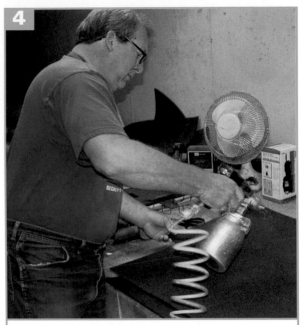

Sammy also makes small (approximately 1/8-inch) alignment holes in the panel board. Since the panel will be made up of a multilayer pattern, the alignment holes will be used to make sure that the pattern lines up correctly.

The entire panel will be covered with one layer of landau foam (available in 1/4- and 3/16-inch thicknesses). The back of the landau foam is sprayed with contact adhesive (applied with a spray gun) and then allowed to become tacky.

Likewise, the panel board is sprayed with contact adhesive and then allowed to become tacky.

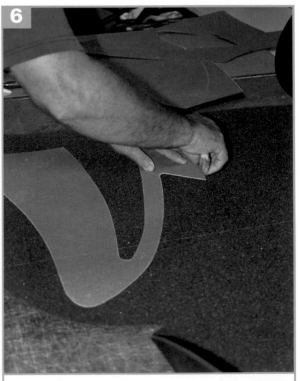

Using the design pattern, Sammy cuts out another piece of landau foam. It will eventually be glued onto the first piece.

7

The landau foam cuts easily with an ordinary utility knife.

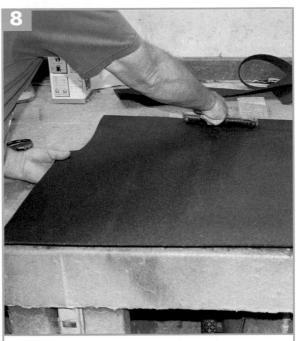

8

The first piece of landau foam that covers the entire panel board is applied. Working from the middle toward the edges, Sammy uses a roller to make sure there are no air bubbles.

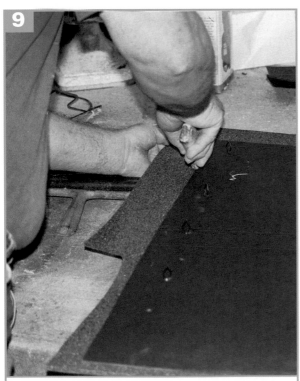

9

After flipping the panel board and foam over, he uses a utility knife to trim off the excess foam.

10

With a sanding board and 80-grit sandpaper, the edges of the panel board are rounded slightly.

11

Sammy locates his reference holes prior to adding more foam. This will ensure that the pattern is the same on both sides.

12

The landau foam has a slick surface, so a sanding block with 80-grit sandpaper is used to rough the surface. This will allow superior adhesion for additional layers of foam.

13

Spray adhesive is applied to the design foam that was cut out earlier. The panel to which it will be applied must be sprayed also.

14

Using the reference holes, the pattern paper is held in place with three awls.

15

Using a piece of chalk, Sammy traces the outline of the pattern onto the foam-covered panel board.

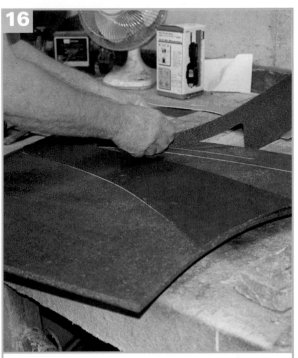

16

The second piece of landau foam is now positioned onto the panel, using the chalk marks for position.

17

The foam is pressed firmly into place, making sure that positioning is correct and that bubbles are eliminated.

18

Three ribs will be added to the lower portion of the panel. Since these are straight, they can be laid out by measuring rather than using a pattern.

19

The back of a small piece of foam is sprayed with contact adhesive.

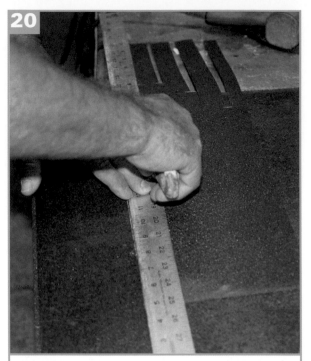

20

After being pressed into place, the three ribs are laid out on the foam.

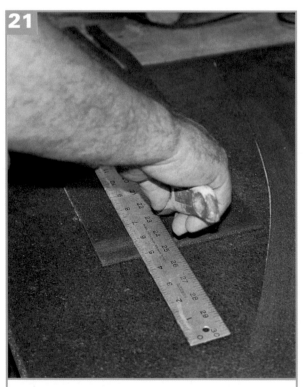

21

The ribs are then cut out using a utility knife and a metal straightedge.

22

After the cuts are made, the leftover foam is peeled away.

The three ribs are then cut to the desired length.

This custom interior panel has more thickness than the original, yet the window garnish molding is the same. Therefore, the panel needs to be trimmed to fit properly. The panel is first slipped into position.

The garnish molding is then installed to show how much of the sculpted panel needs to be recessed.

Sammy traces along the bottom edge of the garnish molding onto the interior panel with a piece of chalk.

27

Sammy removes the panel from the vehicle and cuts through only the first layer of foam. The narrow strip of foam is then peeled off to allow the upholstered panel to fit beneath the garnish molding.

28

The upholstery material can now be cut. The material is unrolled, the panel placed facedown, and the material cut slightly oversize.

29

Spray adhesive is applied to the back of the material (UltraLeather in this case) and to the panel to be covered.

30

With the material facedown on the table, the panel is positioned onto it, making sure that excess material is on all sides.

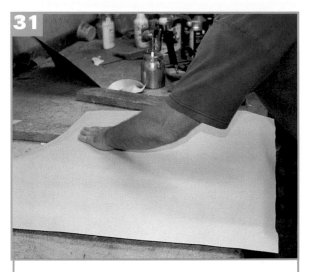

31 With the panel turned right side up, Sammy begins pressing the material into the design.

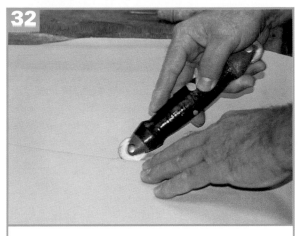

32 Using a screen window installation tool, Sammy works the material into the design portion of the panel. You should start near the center of the panel and work your way out.

33 If the material is too tight to conform to the pattern, a hair dryer can be used to heat the material to make it more workable.

34 With some more work with the screen installation tool, the design is becoming more evident.

35 Some additional heat is required near the ribs at the lower portion of the panel.

INTERIOR

155

36

Pressing the material into place around the ribs takes a bit more time, since they are smaller. Larger, flowing patterns will be easier to work with than smaller, intricate designs.

37

With the material pressed into place around all of the design elements, the flat portion can be pressed into place using a large roller.

38

Excess material is now cut off. Sammy leaves about an inch to wrap around the panel and attach to the back of the panel.

39

The material is now pressed into the recess that will fit beneath the garnish molding.

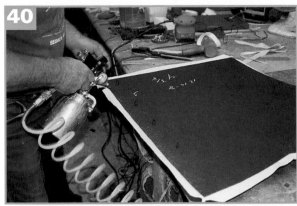

40 More glue is sprayed onto the material that will wrap around to the back of the panel. Notice how the corner in the foreground has been cut. So that the material is not too thick, the corner is cut off; however, a small tab is left to cover the corner of the panel board.

41 The material is now wrapped around the edge and onto the back of the panel board.

42 The finished panel is now installed in the vehicle, making sure that the mounting clips are seated properly.

43 With the panel in place, the window garnish molding is installed to secure it.

Affordable Street Rods
1220 Van Buren
Great Bend, KS 67530
620-792-2836
www.affordablestreetrods.com
Wiring kits and accessories

Billet Specialties, Inc.
500 Shawmut Avenue
La Grange, IL 60525
800-245-5382
www.billetspecialties.com
Billet aluminum wheels, engines, and interior dress-up accessories

Borgeson Universal
187 Commercial Boulevard
Torrington, CT 06790
860-482-8283
www.borgeson.com
Steering shafts, universal joints, couplers, and vibration dampers

Brookville Roadster, Inc.
718 Albert Road
Brookville, OH 45309
937-833-4605
www.brookville-roadster.com
Reproduction steel Ford bodies, parts, and patch panels

Dakota Digital
3421 W. Hovland Avenue
Sioux Falls, SD 57107
888-881-0541
www.dakotadigital.com
Digital gauges

Edelbrock Corporation
2700 California Street
Torrance, CA 90503
310-781-2222
www.edelbrock.com
Engine parts and accessories

Heidt's Hot Rod Shop
111 Kerry Lane
Wauconda, IL 60084
800-841-8188
www.heidts.com
Independent suspension kits and components

March Performance Pulleys
6020 Hix Road
Westland, MI 48185
734-729-9070
www.marchperf.com
Engine pulleys

Morfab Customs
3286 "B" Highway 100
Villa Ridge, MO 63089
636-742-5353
www.morfabcustoms.com
Chassis fabrication and assembly, A/C installation, wiring, turn-key hot rods

Mullins Steering Gears
2876 Sweetwater Avenue, Suite 2
Lake Havasu City, AZ 86406
928-505-3032
www.mullinssteeringgears.com
Steering boxes, columns, and brackets

Pete & Jake's Hot Rod Parts
401 Legend Lane
Peculiar, MO 64078
800-334-7240
www.peteandjakes.com
Chassis, suspension, and brake components

Posies
219 North Duke Street
Hummelstown, PA 17036-1017
717-566-3340
www.posiesrodsandcustoms.com
Suspension components

Super Bell Axle Company
401B Legend Lane
Peculiar, MO 64078
866-758-3300
Dropped axles, spindles, brake kits, and other front-end components

Tanks, Inc.
P.O. Box 400
Clearwater, MN 55320
320-558-6882
Fuel tanks

The Paint Store
2800 High Ridge Boulevard
High Ridge, MO 63049
636-677-1566
Painting products and supplies

Wheel Vintiques
5468 E. Lamona Avenue
Fresno, CA 93727
559-251-6957
www.wheelvintiques.com
Wheels and accessories

Sam Wright Hot Rod Interiors
304 East 1400 Road
Baldwin City, KS 66006
785-594-7430

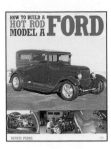
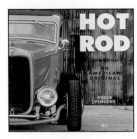
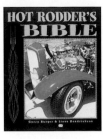

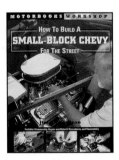
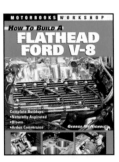
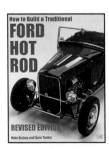